1

BEYOND COMPLIANCE

50 Years Of The Health And Safety At Work Act 1974

Craig McNaughton

Foreword

50 Years ago, the UK set the modern standard for health and safety compliance, passing a bill in parliament that would be seen throughout the world as *the* standard for occupational safety and health, with the sole purpose of protecting persons in the workplace. After half a century of the Health and Safety at Work Etc Act 1974, we find ourselves standing at the intersection of history and progress. This book is not just a retrospective glance; it is a celebration of the journey to foster a culture of safety, well-being, and resilience in our workplaces.

The Health and Safety at Work Act 1974, a pioneering piece of legislation, marked a pivotal moment in time when the collective commitment to the welfare of workers was enshrined in law. In the ensuing decades, this Act has become the cornerstone of a profound transformation, shaping the very essence of how we perceive and prioritize safety within our professional environments.

As we move through the chapters of this book, we explore the evolution of workplace safety, moving beyond the mere adherence to regulations and statutory obligations. This book is a testament to the enduring spirit of innovation, adaptability, and continuous improvement that has defined the progression of safety in the workplace.

The journey, chronicled within these pages, unfolds through the experiences of individuals, organizations, and industries that have embraced the ethos of the Health and Safety at Work Act 1974. It is a journey marked by milestones, challenges surmounted, and lessons learned—a narrative of progress that extends beyond the legal framework, encapsulating the heart and soul of a safer, more humane work environment.

In celebrating this 50th anniversary, "Beyond Compliance" invites readers to reflect on the profound impact of the Act and, more importantly, to envision the future of workplace safety. It challenges us to transcend the confines of mere compliance and embrace a holistic approach that nurtures not only physical well-being but also mental health, inclusivity, and the overall flourishing of individuals within the workplace.

This book serves as both a chronicle and a guide—a reminder of our shared responsibility to create and sustain environments where every worker can thrive. As we honour the past, we cast our gaze forward, recognizing that the journey to a safer workplace is an ongoing, collective endeavour.

May the pages of "Beyond Compliance" inspire, inform, and ignite a renewed commitment to the principles that have guided us for the past 50 years. Here's to the continued evolution of workplace safety and the promise of a future where every person can go to work with the confidence that their well-being is paramount.

Table of Contents

Chapter 7: The Future of Workplace Safety

Conclusion

Appendix

Introduction

Setting the Stage: The Genesis of the Health and Safety at Work Act 1974

In the annals of legislative history, certain moments stand out as pivotal turning points that reshape the fabric of society. The Health and Safety at Work Act 1974, a landmark piece of legislation, is one such moment—a watershed event that transformed the landscape of workplace safety in the United Kingdom.

The journey begins in an era marked by burgeoning industrialisation and a growing awareness of the inherent risks that accompanied progress. From the start of the industrial revolution through to the mid-20th century, surges in industrial activity, accompanied by a rising concern for the well-being of the individuals who toiled in factories, construction sites, and various other workplaces, lead to circumstances in which it became evident that a comprehensive and unified approach was necessary to safeguard the rights and safety of workers.

This book unravels the historical context that prompted the need for a legislative intervention. We delve into the socio-economic conditions of the time, exploring the challenges faced by workers and employers alike. From the hazardous conditions of factories to the rising number of workplace accidents, the imperative for a legislative framework aimed at preserving life, health, and welfare became increasingly apparent.

The following chapters examine the seeds of change sown by predecessors such as the Factories Act 1961 and the Robens Report, which laid the groundwork for a more comprehensive and dynamic approach to occupational health and safety. It delves into the debates, discussions, and societal shifts that ultimately culminated in the passage of the Health and Safety at Work Act 1974.

As we traverse this historical landscape, readers will gain insights into the individuals, events, and catalytic moments that coalesced to bring about this transformative piece of legislation. This text serves as a backdrop, illuminating the path that led to the birth of the HASAWA 1974—a path paved with the collective consciousness of a nation recognizing the intrinsic value of human life in the workplace.

The genesis of the Health and Safety at Work Act 1974 is not just a historical curiosity; it is a testament to the enduring commitment to the well-being of those who contribute to the progress and prosperity of our society. The progression from the first piece of true safety legislation presented to parliament by Sir Robert Peel in 1802, to the modern act itself is outlined below.

Health and Morals of Apprentices Act 1802
- Also known as the Cotton Mills Regulation Act, this was the first legislative attempt to improve conditions for apprentices working in cotton mills.

Factory Acts 1833
- This act limited the working hours for children (ages 9-13) and created factory inspectors.

Mines and Collieries Act 1842
- Although not a Factory Act, it was an important piece of legislation that regulated conditions for workers in mines and collieries.

Factory Act 1844
- This act further restricted working hours and included more industries, including women and young persons.

Factory Act 1847
- Addressed issues of sanitation and ventilation in factories.

Factory Act 1850
- Extended restrictions on working hours to women.

Factory Act 1878
- Set further regulations on hours and conditions, and introduced the concept of a "certifying surgeon."

Factory and Workshop Act 1901
- Consolidated previous factory legislation and introduced new requirements.

Factory and Workshop Act 1922
- Provided for the control and inspection of machinery, improved sanitation, and restricted working hours for women and young persons.

Factories Act 1937
- Introduced provisions for welfare facilities and extended the scope of regulation.

Factories Act 1959
- Modernized and consolidated factory legislation, addressing issues like health, safety, and welfare.

Health and Safety at Work Act 1974(c. 37):
- A comprehensive piece of legislation that marked a shift from industry-specific regulations to a more general framework, focusing on the health, safety, and welfare of all employees.

These acts represent a progression in the development of legislation aimed at improving working conditions and protecting the well-being of workers in the United Kingdom. The Health and Safety at Work Act 1974 is a culmination of these efforts, providing a more comprehensive and unified approach to workplace safety.

Chapter 1: Origins

The timeline to compliance

Overview of the Health and Morals of Apprentices Act 1802

 The Health and Morals of Apprentices Act was introduced by Sir Robert Peel, who had become concerned in the issue after a 1784 outbreak of a "malignant fever" at one of his cotton mills, which he later blamed on 'gross mismanagement' by his subordinates. Passed in 1802, this act represented a pioneering piece of legislation in the United Kingdom that sought to address the harsh working conditions faced by apprentices, the majority of which were children, particularly those employed in cotton mills during the early stages of the Industrial Revolution. Commonly known as the Cotton Mills Regulation Act, this legislation marked an early acknowledgment of the need to protect the welfare of individuals, particularly young apprentices, within industrial settings.

Key Provisions:

Limitation of Working Hours:
- The Act aimed to regulate the working hours of apprentices in cotton mills. It stipulated that no apprentice under the age of 21 should work more than 12 hours a day.

Nightwork Restrictions:
- The Act prohibited nightwork for apprentices, recognizing the detrimental impact that extended and nocturnal working hours had on the health and well-being of young workers.

Moral and Physical Care:
- Emphasizing a concern for the holistic well-being of apprentices, the Act included provisions related to moral and physical care. Employers were expected to provide apprentices with suitable accommodation, clothing, and sufficient food.

Medical Inspection:
- The legislation introduced the concept of medical inspections by requiring factory owners to arrange for a yearly visit by a surgeon or physician. This provision aimed at ensuring the health and fitness of apprentices.

Education and Religious Instruction:
- Employers were obligated to provide a basic level of education and religious instruction for apprentices, recognizing the importance of intellectual and moral development.

Significance:

Humanitarian Concerns:
- The Health and Morals of Apprentices Act 1802 was a response to growing concerns about the deplorable working conditions, especially for young apprentices. It reflected a nascent understanding of the need to balance industrial progress with humanitarian considerations.

Early Regulation of Factory Conditions:
- While the scope of this legislation was limited to cotton mills and apprentices, it laid the groundwork for subsequent Factory Acts that would extend protections to a broader range of workers and industries.

Shift Toward Legislative Intervention:
- The Act represented a significant departure from the prevailing laissez-faire economic ideology, signalling a growing recognition of the state's role in regulating and ensuring humane working conditions.

The Health and Morals of Apprentices Act 1802, though modest in scope, played a crucial role in initiating a trajectory of labour legislation that would evolve over the years, eventually leading to more comprehensive laws addressing workplace safety, health, and welfare in the United Kingdom. It stands as a testament to the evolving societal attitudes toward the treatment of workers during a transformative period in industrial history.

Overview of the Factory Acts 1833

The Factory Acts of 1833 marked a significant milestone in the history of labour regulation in the United Kingdom, representing a comprehensive legislative response to the widespread exploitation and unsafe working conditions prevalent during the early stages of the Industrial Revolution. Enacted during the reign of William IV, these acts aimed to address the welfare of workers, particularly children, and laid the foundation for subsequent factory legislation.

Key Provisions:

Limitation of Working Hours for Children:
- The Factory Act of 1833 introduced a critical limitation on the working hours of children (ages 9-13) in textile factories. It restricted their working hours to a maximum of 48 hours per week, divided over six days.

Appointment of Factory Inspectors:
- To enforce the provisions of the Act, factory inspectors were appointed to monitor compliance and ensure that employers adhered to the prescribed working conditions.

Educational Requirements:

- The legislation recognized the importance of education for child laborers. It mandated that a portion of each working day be dedicated to education, with a minimum of two hours of schooling per day.

Factory Registers:

- Employers were required to maintain registers that documented the names, ages, and hours of work for all child labourers. This measure aimed to provide transparency and accountability.

Prohibition of Nightwork for Young Persons:

- The Factory Act extended its protective provisions to young persons (ages 13-18), prohibiting nightwork and establishing a maximum 12-hour working day.

Health and Safety Measures:

- The legislation included provisions related to the cleanliness and ventilation of factories, recognizing the importance of a safe and healthy working environment.

Penalties for Non-Compliance:

- The Factory Acts of 1833 imposed penalties, including fines, for employers who failed to comply with the established regulations. This reinforced the enforcement mechanisms to ensure the well-being of workers.

Significance:

Child Labor Reform:
- The Factory Acts of 1833 were instrumental in addressing the widespread exploitation of child labour in textile factories. By setting limits on working hours and mandating education, the legislation aimed to protect the vulnerable population of young workers.

Introduction of Factory Inspection:
- The appointment of factory inspectors marked the beginning of systematic oversight and enforcement of labour laws, ensuring that employers adhered to the prescribed standards.

Shift Toward Protective Legislation:
- These acts signalled a significant shift in public policy toward protective labour legislation, reflecting a growing awareness of the need to balance industrial progress with humane working conditions.

Precursor to Subsequent Legislation:
- The Factory Acts of 1833 laid the groundwork for future labour laws, establishing a precedent for the regulation of working conditions, limitations on working hours, and the importance of education for child workers.

The Factory Acts of 1833 represented a crucial step in the ongoing evolution of labour regulation, setting the stage for subsequent legislation that would continue to refine and expand protections for workers in the United Kingdom.

Overview of the Mines and Collieries Act 1842

The Mines and Collieries Act of 1842 was a pioneering piece of legislation in the United Kingdom aimed at improving working conditions and safety standards in mines and collieries during the Industrial Revolution. Born out of a growing awareness of the hazardous and exploitative conditions faced by mine workers, this act represented a significant step towards the protection of the physical well-being of those employed in the mining industry.

Key Provisions:

Regulation of Working Hours:
- The Mines and Collieries Act of 1842 set limits on the working hours of women and children in mines. It prohibited the employment of females and boys under the age of 10 underground.

Appointment of Inspectors:
- The legislation established the appointment of inspectors to enforce the provisions of the Act. These inspectors were tasked with monitoring compliance with regulations and ensuring the well-being of workers.

Ventilation and Safety Measures:

- Recognizing the perilous working conditions in mines, the act included provisions for improved ventilation to address issues such as the accumulation of dangerous gases. It also emphasized the importance of maintaining safety standards.

Prohibition of Employment of Women and Boys in Certain Jobs:

- The act specified certain jobs that were deemed too dangerous for the employment of women and boys, further protecting these vulnerable groups from hazardous tasks.

Record-Keeping Requirements:

- Mine owners were required to keep accurate records of the ages of workers and their hours of work, providing transparency and aiding in the enforcement of regulations.

Significance:

Protection of Vulnerable Workers:

- The Mines and Collieries Act of 1842 addressed the exploitation of women and young boys in the mining industry by setting age limits and regulating working hours, offering a level of protection for these vulnerable groups.

Focus on Safety:

- By introducing measures to improve ventilation and specifying certain jobs deemed too dangerous for certain workers, the legislation aimed to enhance safety standards in mines, acknowledging the inherent risks of mining work.

Inspectorate System:

- The act established a system of inspection, laying the foundation for a broader system of regulatory oversight. Inspectors played a crucial role in ensuring compliance and reporting on the conditions of mines.

Early Industrial Safety Legislation:

- The Mines and Collieries Act of 1842 was one of the earliest instances of industrial safety legislation, reflecting a growing understanding of the need for legal safeguards to protect workers in hazardous occupations.

While the Mines and Collieries Act of 1842 represented a significant step forward in the regulation of mines, it was followed by subsequent legislation that further refined and expanded protections for workers in the mining industry in the years to come.

Overview of the Factory Act 1844

The Factory Act of 1844 was a critical piece of legislation in the United Kingdom, building upon earlier Factory Acts, and aimed at refining and extending protections for workers, particularly women and young persons, during the Industrial Revolution. This act represented a continued effort to address the working conditions and hours of labour in factories, recognizing the need for ongoing regulation to safeguard the well-being of the labour force.

Key Provisions:

Reduction in Working Hours:
- One of the primary provisions of the Factory Act 1844 was the reduction of the maximum working hours for women and young persons (ages 13-18) in textile factories. It established a 12-hour working day, from 6 a.m. to 6 p.m., with two hours allocated for meal breaks.

Extension of Legislation to Other Industries:
- The scope of the Factory Act 1844 was expanded to include non-textile factories, recognizing that the protective measures previously implemented needed to be extended to a broader range of industries.

Half-Day on Saturday:
- The act introduced the concept of a half-day on Saturday for women and young persons, further restricting the total weekly working hours.

Appointment of Certifying Surgeons:
- The legislation introduced the requirement for certifying surgeons, who were responsible for examining young persons and women to ensure they were fit for employment in a factory. This was a measure to protect the health of the workers.

Records of Accidents and Injuries:
- Factory owners were required to keep records of accidents and injuries, promoting transparency and providing insight into the safety conditions within the workplace.

Significance:

Continued Reduction of Working Hours:
- The Factory Act of 1844 continued the trend of reducing working hours for certain segments of the workforce, particularly women and young persons, reflecting an ongoing commitment to improving labor conditions.

Expansion of Protections to Non-Textile Industries:
- By extending the protective measures to non-textile factories, the legislation acknowledged that the issues addressed in previous acts were not exclusive to specific industries, recognizing the need for uniform regulation.

Health Protections:

- The appointment of certifying surgeons and the requirement for accident records underscored a growing concern for the health and well-being of workers. The act aimed to prevent exploitation and ensure that individuals were fit for the demands of factory work.

Enhanced Transparency:

- The Factory Act of 1844 promoted transparency by mandating record-keeping of accidents and injuries. This information was crucial for understanding and addressing the safety challenges within factories.

The Factory Act 1844 contributed to the evolution of labour legislation, representing a step forward in the ongoing effort to establish a balance between industrial progress and the protection of workers' rights and well-being. It foreshadowed subsequent legislation that would continue to refine and expand these protections in the years to come.

Overview of the Factory Act 1847

The Factory Act of 1847 was a significant piece of legislation in the United Kingdom, building upon earlier Factory Acts, and aimed at further refining and extending protections for workers during the Industrial Revolution. This act, like its predecessors, was part of ongoing efforts to address and improve the conditions of labour in factories, with a particular focus on women and young persons.

Key Provisions:

Further Reduction in Working Hours:
- The Factory Act of 1847 continued the trend of reducing working hours for women and young persons (ages 13-18) in textile factories. It further restricted the maximum working hours to 10 hours per day, with a total of 58 hours per week.

Extension of Legislation to Non-Textile Factories:
- Similar to the Factory Act of 1844, this legislation extended its protective measures to non-textile factories, recognizing the need for uniform regulation across various industrial sectors.

Meal Breaks:
- The act introduced the requirement for a one-hour meal break during the working day, emphasizing the importance of providing workers with adequate rest and sustenance.

Appointment of Factory Inspectors:

- Factory inspectors were appointed to enforce the provisions of the Act. These inspectors played a crucial role in monitoring compliance, conducting inspections, and ensuring that employers adhered to the prescribed standards.

Increased Certifying Surgeon Oversight:

- The legislation strengthened the role of certifying surgeons by requiring them to provide a medical certificate to each young person and woman they examined. This added layer of scrutiny aimed to ensure the health and fitness of workers for factory employment.

Significance:

Continued Reduction of Working Hours:

- The Factory Act of 1847 maintained the momentum of reducing working hours for women and young persons, reflecting an ongoing commitment to improve the conditions and well-being of the labour force.

Expansion of Protections to Non-Textile Industries:

- Similar to the Factory Act of 1844, this legislation extended its protective measures to non-textile factories, recognizing that issues addressed in previous acts were relevant across various industries.

Focus on Health and Well-being:

- The act emphasized the importance of providing workers with adequate breaks for meals and rest, signalling a growing awareness of the relationship between working conditions and the health and well-being of employees.

Inspectorate System Strengthened:

- The appointment of factory inspectors marked a strengthening of the inspectorate system, contributing to more effective enforcement of regulations and ensuring employers adhered to the prescribed standards.

The Factory Act of 1847, building upon the foundation laid by earlier legislation, played a crucial role in shaping the evolving landscape of labour regulation. It reflected an ongoing commitment to strike a balance between industrial progress and the protection of workers' rights, health, and well-being during a transformative period in history.

Overview of the Factory Act 1850

The Factory Act of 1850 was a pivotal piece of legislation in the United Kingdom, representing a continued evolution of labour laws during the Industrial Revolution. Building upon the preceding Factory Acts, this legislation aimed to further refine and extend protections for workers, with a focus on restricting working hours and enhancing conditions in factories.

Key Provisions:

Reduction in Working Hours:
- The Factory Act of 1850 continued the trend of reducing working hours for women and young persons (ages 13-18) in textile factories. It limited the maximum working hours to 10 hours per day, with a total of 58 hours per week.

Extension of Legislation to Non-Textile Factories:
- Similar to previous Factory Acts, this legislation extended its protective measures to non-textile factories, recognizing the importance of applying uniform regulations across various industrial sectors.

Meal Breaks and Rest Periods:
- The act reinforced the necessity of providing workers with adequate breaks, including a one-hour meal break and two shorter rest periods during the working day. This underscored the importance of rest and sustenance for the well-being of workers.

Appointment of Factory Inspectors:

- The Factory Act of 1850 continued the practice of appointing factory inspectors to enforce the provisions of the Act. These inspectors played a vital role in overseeing compliance, conducting inspections, and ensuring that employers adhered to the prescribed standards.

Increased Certifying Surgeon Oversight:

- The role of certifying surgeons was further emphasized, with increased scrutiny over the medical certificates they provided. This measure aimed to ensure a more thorough examination of the health and fitness of workers for factory employment.

Significance:

Continued Emphasis on Working Hours:

- The Factory Act of 1850 maintained a focus on the reduction of working hours, recognizing the need to balance industrial productivity with the well-being of workers.

Comprehensive Regulation Across Industries:

- Extending protective measures to non-textile factories reaffirmed the understanding that the issues addressed in the legislation were not industry-specific but applied universally to various industrial sectors.

Promotion of Worker Well-being:

- The provisions related to meal breaks and rest periods underscored a growing awareness of the importance of worker well-being and the need to provide sufficient opportunities for rest and sustenance during the workday.

Strengthening of Enforcement Mechanisms:

- The appointment of factory inspectors and the emphasis on certifying surgeons contributed to the strengthening of enforcement mechanisms, ensuring more effective oversight and adherence to prescribed standards.

The Factory Act of 1850, building upon the foundations laid by its predecessors, exemplifies an ongoing commitment to improving labour conditions and protecting the rights of workers during a period of industrial transformation. It reflects the evolving understanding of the relationship between working conditions and the health and well-being of the labour force in the 19th century.

Overview of the Factory Act 1878

The Factory Act of 1878 was a significant piece of legislation in the United Kingdom, building upon the foundation of earlier Factory Acts, and aimed at further refining and extending protections for workers during the Industrial Revolution. This legislation responded to the changing landscape of industrialization and addressed emerging challenges, focusing on improving working conditions and safety standards.

Key Provisions:

Limitation of Working Hours:
- The Factory Act of 1878 continued the trend of restricting working hours for women and young persons (ages 13-18) in textile factories. It limited the maximum working hours to 10 hours per day, with a total of 56 hours per week.

Expansion of Legislation to Non-Textile Factories:
- The protective measures of the Factory Act were extended to non-textile factories, recognizing the importance of providing uniform regulations across various industrial sectors.

Appointment of Factory Inspectors:
- The act continued the practice of appointing factory inspectors to enforce its provisions. These inspectors played a crucial role in monitoring compliance, conducting inspections, and ensuring that employers adhered to the prescribed standards.

Enhanced Certification Requirements:
- The legislation strengthened the certification process by requiring factory surgeons to examine workers at least once a year and issue a certificate specifying the worker's fitness for employment.

Prohibition of Underground Work for Women and Young Persons:
- The act prohibited the employment of women and young persons underground in mines and certain other specified processes, recognizing the particular risks associated with such work.

Increased Protections for Night Workers:
- Special protections were introduced for night workers, including the limitation of working hours and additional regulations to safeguard their health and well-being.

Significance:

Continued Focus on Working Hours:
- The Factory Act of 1878 maintained a focus on the reduction of working hours for women and young persons, reflecting the ongoing commitment to balancing industrial productivity with the health and well-being of the workforce.

Wider Application Across Industries:
- Extending protective measures to non-textile factories and addressing underground work in certain processes demonstrated an understanding that industrial regulations should be comprehensive and apply universally.

Strengthening of Certification Process:
- The enhanced certification requirements reflected a commitment to ensuring a thorough examination of workers' health, providing a layer of protection against exploitation and unhealthy working conditions.

Special Protections for Night Workers:
- The inclusion of specific provisions for night workers recognized the unique challenges and health considerations associated with nighttime employment.

The Factory Act of 1878 represented a continuation of efforts to improve working conditions and protect the rights of workers in the evolving industrial landscape. By addressing emerging challenges and expanding the scope of regulations, the legislation contributed to the ongoing evolution of labor laws in the 19th century.

Overview of the Factory and Workshop Act 1901

The Factory and Workshop Act of 1901 was a significant piece of legislation in the United Kingdom, representing a culmination of efforts to address and regulate working conditions in factories and workshops. This comprehensive act aimed to enhance the protection of workers by refining and expanding upon the provisions of earlier Factory Acts.

Key Provisions:

Definition of Factory and Workshop:
- The Factory and Workshop Act of 1901 provided clearer definitions of what constituted a factory and a workshop, ensuring that regulatory protections were appropriately applied to different types of workplaces.

Limitation of Working Hours:
- The act continued the trend of restricting working hours for women and young persons (ages 13-18) in factories and workshops. It maintained the limit of 10 hours per day and 56 hours per week.

Improved Safety and Health Standards:
- The legislation introduced enhanced safety and health standards, including provisions for the proper fencing and guarding of machinery to prevent accidents, as well as requirements for adequate ventilation and cleanliness in workplaces.

Appointment of Certifying Surgeons:

- The act continued the requirement for certifying surgeons, who were responsible for examining workers and issuing medical certificates to determine their fitness for employment.

Protection for Home Workers:

- The Factory and Workshop Act extended protections to home workers engaged in certain processes, recognizing that work undertaken outside traditional factory settings also required regulatory oversight.

Appointment of Factory and Workshop Inspectors:

- The legislation appointed factory and workshop inspectors to enforce compliance with its provisions. These inspectors played a crucial role in conducting inspections, ensuring adherence to standards, and promoting a safe and healthy working environment.

Annual Leave Entitlement:

- The act introduced the provision of annual leave for workers, marking a recognition of the importance of providing workers with opportunities for rest and recreation.

Significance:

Holistic Approach to Regulation:

- The Factory and Workshop Act of 1901 took a comprehensive and holistic approach to regulation, addressing not only working hours but also safety, health, and the conditions of various types of workplaces.

Adaptation to Changing Work Environments:

- By extending protections to home workers and incorporating clearer definitions, the legislation demonstrated an awareness of the changing landscape of work and the need to adapt regulations accordingly.

Focus on Safety and Health Standards:

- The introduction of enhanced safety and health standards reflected an increased emphasis on creating workplaces that prioritized the well-being and safety of the workforce.

Introduction of Annual Leave:

- The provision for annual leave recognized the importance of providing workers with time for rest and recreation, contributing to the overall welfare of the labor force.

The Factory and Workshop Act of 1901 marked a significant step forward in the ongoing evolution of labor laws, addressing emerging challenges and adapting to changes in the industrial landscape. Its provisions laid the groundwork for a more comprehensive and nuanced approach to regulating working conditions in the 20th century.

Overview of the Factory and Workshop Act 1922

The Factory and Workshop Act of 1922 was a key piece of legislation in the United Kingdom, representing a continued effort to regulate and improve working conditions in factories and workshops. This act built upon the foundations of earlier legislation and introduced new provisions aimed at addressing the evolving needs of the industrial workforce.

Key Provisions:

Limitation of Working Hours:
- The Factory and Workshop Act of 1922 continued the tradition of limiting working hours for women and young persons (ages 13-18) in factories and workshops. It maintained the 10-hour maximum working day and 56-hour maximum working week.

Annual Leave Entitlement:
- Building on the provisions introduced by the 1901 Act, the legislation included further details regarding annual leave entitlement for workers, specifying the duration and conditions for taking leave.

Night Work Restrictions:

- The act introduced additional restrictions on night work for women and young persons, recognizing the potential adverse effects on health and well-being. It specified limitations on the hours during which night work was permitted.

Improved Safety and Health Standards:

- The legislation strengthened safety and health standards by introducing more detailed requirements for the fencing and guarding of machinery, ensuring workplace cleanliness, and promoting overall safety measures.

Provisions for Welfare Facilities:

- The Factory and Workshop Act of 1922 included provisions for the provision of welfare facilities in factories and workshops. This encompassed requirements for adequate washing facilities, drinking water, and spaces for meals.

Appointment of Factory Inspectors:

- The act continued the appointment of factory inspectors to enforce compliance with its provisions. These inspectors were responsible for conducting regular inspections, ensuring adherence to standards, and promoting a safe and healthy working environment.

Regulation of Dangerous Processes:

- Specific provisions were introduced to regulate dangerous processes, emphasizing the need for additional precautions and safety measures in workplaces involved in particularly hazardous activities.

Significance:

Continued Emphasis on Working Hours:

- The Factory and Workshop Act of 1922 maintained the focus on limiting working hours, recognizing the importance of balancing productivity with the health and well-being of workers.

Expansion of Welfare Provisions:

- The introduction of provisions for welfare facilities marked an increased emphasis on providing workers with a conducive and hygienic working environment, contributing to their overall well-being.

Enhanced Safety and Health Standards:

- The strengthening of safety and health standards reflected an ongoing commitment to creating workplaces that prioritized the prevention of accidents and the protection of workers.

Night Work Restrictions for Women and Young Persons:

- The specific restrictions on night work acknowledged the potential risks associated with such schedules, aligning with a growing understanding of the importance of regulating working hours to safeguard worker health.

The Factory and Workshop Act of 1922 played a vital role in shaping the regulatory framework for workplaces in the early 20th century. Its provisions addressed emerging challenges and reinforced the commitment to ensuring the safety, health, and welfare of the industrial workforce in the evolving industrial landscape.

Overview of the Factories Act 1937

The Factories Act 1937 was a significant piece of legislation in the United Kingdom, consolidating and updating previous factory legislation to improve and streamline the regulatory framework for industrial workplaces. This act represented a comprehensive effort to address the evolving needs of the workforce, enhance safety standards, and adapt to changing industrial conditions.

Key Provisions:

Consolidation of Previous Legislation:

- The Factories Act 1937 consolidated and replaced earlier factory legislation, bringing together various provisions from Acts dating back to the 19th century. This consolidation aimed to provide a more coherent and accessible set of regulations for factory owners and workers.

Limitation of Working Hours:
- The act continued the tradition of limiting working hours for women and young persons (ages 16-18) in factories. It set the maximum working day at 9 hours and the maximum working week at 48 hours.

Regulation of Night Work:
- The legislation included specific provisions for night work, regulating the hours during which women and young persons could be employed. This aimed to mitigate the potential health and safety risks associated with night shifts.

Welfare Facilities and Safety Standards:
- The Factories Act 1937 introduced detailed provisions regarding welfare facilities in factories, including sanitary arrangements, ventilation, and lighting. It also reinforced safety standards, addressing issues such as machinery safety, fencing, and protective measures.

Health Examinations and Certificates:
- The act continued the requirement for health examinations and certificates for young persons, ensuring that workers were fit for the demands of factory employment.

Appointment of Factory Inspectors:

- Factory inspectors were appointed to enforce the provisions of the Factories Act 1937. These inspectors played a crucial role in conducting inspections, ensuring compliance with standards, and promoting a safe and healthy working environment.

Prohibition of Dangerous Machines for Certain Workers:

- Specific provisions were introduced to prohibit certain classes of workers from operating dangerous machinery, enhancing protections for those particularly vulnerable to workplace hazards.

Significance:

Consolidation and Clarity:

- The Factories Act 1937 brought clarity and coherence to the regulatory landscape by consolidating and updating previous legislation. This made it easier for employers and workers to understand and adhere to the legal framework.

Emphasis on Welfare Facilities:

- The detailed provisions regarding welfare facilities underscored a growing awareness of the importance of creating a conducive and hygienic working environment to promote the well-being of the workforce.

Adaptation to Changing Conditions:
- The legislation adapted to changing industrial conditions by introducing specific regulations for night work and addressing new challenges associated with evolving technologies and machinery.

Continued Focus on Working Hours:
- The Factories Act 1937 maintained the emphasis on limiting working hours, recognizing the importance of a balanced approach to ensure the health and well-being of workers.

The Factories Act 1937 represented a crucial stage in the ongoing evolution of factory legislation, responding to the needs of the time and providing a comprehensive regulatory framework for industrial workplaces in the mid-20th century. Its provisions contributed to the promotion of worker safety, health, and welfare during a period of industrial transformation.

The Factories Act 1959 and Factories Bill 1961

The Factories Act 1959 marked a significant milestone in the United Kingdom's factory legislation, consolidating and updating previous laws to address the changing landscape of industrial work. The Factories Bill 1961 was introduced as part of the legislative process to enact the provisions outlined in the Factories Act 1959. Together, these legislative measures aimed to modernize regulations, improve working conditions, and ensure the safety and well-being of factory workers.

Key Provisions of the Factories Act 1959:

Scope and Definitions:

- The Act expanded and clarified the scope of previous factory legislation, providing clear definitions and distinctions for different types of factories and workplaces.

Limitation of Working Hours:

- Building on earlier legislation, the Factories Act 1959 continued to limit working hours for women and young persons (ages 16-18) in factories. It set the standard working week at 48 hours.

Night Work Regulations:

- The Act introduced specific regulations governing night work, addressing concerns related to the potential health and safety risks associated with nighttime employment.

Welfare Facilities and Safety Standards:

- The legislation reinforced and updated provisions related to welfare facilities, sanitary arrangements, ventilation, and safety standards in factories. It aimed to create a safer and healthier working environment.

Health Examinations and Certificates:

- The requirement for health examinations and certificates for young persons was continued, ensuring that workers were physically fit for the demands of factory employment.

Key Provisions of the Factories Bill 1961:

Transition from Bill to Act:

- The Factories Bill 1961 represented the proposed legislation that was later enacted as the Factories Act 1959. It went through the legislative process, including parliamentary discussions, amendments, and approvals, before becoming law.

Incorporation of Amendments:

- The Factories Bill 1961 incorporated amendments and changes to existing legislation, reflecting the evolving needs of the industrial workforce and responding to emerging challenges.

Significance:

Modernization and Clarity:

- The Factories Act 1959, supported by the Factories Bill 1961, aimed to modernize and simplify the regulatory framework, providing greater clarity for both employers and workers regarding their rights and responsibilities.

Adaptation to Changing Conditions:

- The legislation adapted to changing industrial conditions by addressing concerns related to night work and updating safety and health standards to align with technological advancements and evolving work practices.

Continued Emphasis on Welfare:

- The provisions related to welfare facilities underscored an ongoing commitment to creating workplaces that prioritized the well-being of the workforce, acknowledging the importance of adequate facilities for health and comfort.

Consolidation and Streamlining:

- The Factories Act 1959 and the Factories Bill 1961 contributed to the consolidation and streamlining of factory legislation, making it more accessible and effective in addressing the needs of the time.

The Factories Act 1959, along with the supporting Factories Bill 1961, played a crucial role in shaping the regulatory landscape for factories in the UK during the mid-20th century. These legislative measures represented a commitment to worker safety, health, and welfare while adapting to the changing nature of industrial work.

A Legislative Milestone: Unpacking the Core Tenets of the Health and Safety at Work Act 1974

As we traverse the historical landscape that led to the enactment of the Health and Safety at Work Act 1974 (HSWA 1974), it becomes imperative to delve into the very essence of this landmark legislation.

"A Legislative Milestone" is a chapter dedicated to unraveling the intricacies of the Act, understanding its core tenets, and appreciating the revolutionary impact it has had on the landscape of occupational health and safety.

The HSWA 1974 was not merely a set of regulations; it represented a paradigm shift in how societies approached the welfare of individuals in the workplace. What follows will hopefully serve as a guide, offering readers a comprehensive understanding of the Act's fundamental principles and objectives.

Let's begin by dissecting the overarching goals that shaped the HASAWA 1974. From its inception, the Act aimed to create a framework that went beyond mere compliance, aspiring to instill a culture of proactive risk management and continuous improvement. We explore the Act's commitment to ensuring the health, safety, and welfare of individuals at work, from the shop floor to the executive suite.

Section 1. This section is the preliminary, which sets the boundaries to which the act relates.

Section 2 of the Health and Safety at Work Act 1974 outlines the general duties of employers to ensure the health, safety, and welfare of their employees. This section establishes fundamental principles that employers are obligated to follow to create and maintain a safe working environment. General duties must be performed "So far as is reasonably practicable", whereby the benefit of risk reduction outweighs the time, cost and effort of putting it into effect.

Ensuring Health, Safety, and Welfare (Section 2(1)):

Employers have a duty to ensure, so far as is reasonably practicable, the health, safety, and welfare at work of all their employees.

Safe Systems of Work (Section 2(2)(a)):

Employers are required to provide and maintain systems of work that are safe and without risks to health.

Safe Plant and Equipment (Section 2(2)(b)):

Employers must provide and maintain a safe working environment, including safe machinery, equipment, and tools.

Safe Handling, Storage, and Transport of Articles and Substances (Section 2(2)(c)):

Employers must ensure the safe handling, storage, and transport of articles and substances that employees use in the course of their work.

Adequate Training, Information, Instruction, and Supervision (Section 2(2)(d)):

Employers are responsible for providing employees with adequate training, information, instruction, and supervision to ensure their health and safety.

Safe Access and Egress (Section 2(2)(e)):

Employers must provide and maintain safe access to and egress from the workplace. This includes ensuring that exits are clearly marked and accessible.

Safe Working Environment (Section 2(2)(f)):

Employers have a duty to provide and maintain a working environment that is safe, without risks to health, and with adequate facilities.

Risk Assessments (Section 2(3)):

Employers are required to conduct risk assessments to identify potential hazards in the workplace and take measures to eliminate or control these risks.

Health and Safety Policy (Section 2(3A)):

Employers with five or more employees must have a written health and safety policy that outlines the organization's commitment to health and safety and the arrangements in place to achieve this.

Consultation with Employees (Section 2(4)):

Employers are obligated to consult with employees or their representatives on matters related to health and safety. This may include appointing safety representatives and establishing safety committees.

Coordination and Cooperation (Section 2(5)):

Employers must coordinate their efforts with other employers or self-employed individuals sharing the same workplace to ensure that health and safety obligations are met.

The overarching principle of Section 2 is that employers have a legal duty to take all reasonably practicable steps to protect the health, safety, and welfare of their employees. This involves a comprehensive approach that includes risk assessments, proper training, provision of necessary information, and ongoing consultation with employees to create and maintain a safe working environment. Non-compliance with these duties may result in legal consequences, including enforcement action by regulatory authorities.

Section 3 of the Health and Safety at Work Act 1974 outlines the general duties of employers and self-employed individuals concerning persons who are not their employees. This section emphasizes the responsibility of employers and self-employed individuals to ensure that their work activities do not pose risks to the health and safety of individuals who may be affected by their operations but are not direct employees.

Scope of Duty:

Section 3 places a duty on employers and self-employed individuals to conduct their work activities in a manner that ensures, so far as is reasonably practicable, that persons who are not their employees are not exposed to risks to their health and safety.

Reasonably Practicable Measures:

The duty imposed by Section 3 is subject to the concept of "reasonably practicable." This means that employers and self-employed individuals are expected to take measures to mitigate risks, but these measures should be proportionate to the level of risk and the resources available.

Specific Measures:

Employers and self-employed individuals must take specific measures to safeguard the health and safety of non-employees. This may include implementing safe systems of work, providing adequate information and training, and putting in place physical safeguards to prevent accidents.

Information and Training:

Employers and self-employed individuals are required to provide information and training to non-employees who may be exposed to risks. This is crucial for ensuring that individuals are aware of potential hazards and understand how to protect themselves.

Coordination with Other Duty Holders:

Section 3 acknowledges that in situations where multiple parties share responsibility for a workplace or activity, coordination is necessary. Employers and self-employed individuals must cooperate with other duty holders to ensure the health and safety of all individuals involved.

Examples of Non-Employees:

Non-employees covered by this section may include visitors to a workplace, customers, clients, contractors, and members of the public. The duty extends to anyone who may be affected by the work activities but is not under a direct employment relationship with the employer or self-employed person.

Consideration of Work Activities:

The duty under Section 3 requires employers and self-employed individuals to consider the nature of their work activities and the potential impact on the health and safety of non-employees. This includes activities carried out on or off the employer's premises.

Risk Assessment and Mitigation:

As with the general duties to employees, employers and self-employed individuals are expected to conduct risk assessments to identify potential hazards and take appropriate measures to mitigate these risks.

In summary, Section 3 of the Health and Safety at Work Act 1974 emphasizes the broader responsibility of employers and self-employed individuals to ensure the health and safety of persons other than their employees. This duty reflects a recognition that work activities can have an impact beyond the direct workforce, and measures should be taken to protect the health and safety of all individuals who may be affected.

Section 4 of the Health and Safety at Work Act 1974 outlines the general duties of persons concerned with premises to persons other than their employees. This section is crucial in recognizing that workplace safety extends beyond employees to include individuals who may be affected by the activities conducted on the premises.

Scope of the Duty:

This section places a duty on individuals or entities who have control over premises to ensure that the health and safety of individuals other than their employees are not adversely affected by the conduct of their activities.

Definition of "Persons Other than Their Employees":

This includes visitors, customers, contractors, or any individuals who are not employed by the person or organization controlling the premises.

Safe Condition and Safe Access:

Those in control of premises must ensure that the premises are safe for individuals other than their employees.

This involves maintaining the premises in a safe condition and providing safe access to and egress from the premises.

Warning of Risks:

Persons in control of premises are required to provide adequate warnings of any risks or hazards that individuals other than their employees might encounter while on the premises.

Non-Employees Not to be Exposed to Risks:

Individuals who are not employees should not be exposed to risks to their health and safety that are related to the conduct of activities on the premises.

Duty to Non-Employees in Vicinity of Premises:

The duty extends to individuals in the vicinity of the premises, meaning that risks emanating from the premises should not pose a threat to the health and safety of those in the surrounding area.

Responsibility for Activities on the Premises:

Persons in control of premises are responsible for the safety of individuals other than their employees in relation to the activities conducted on the premises.

Information and Instruction:

Providing necessary information and instructions to non-employees about any risks or safety measures is part of the duty. This may include notifying visitors of emergency exits, potential hazards, or safety procedures.

Ensuring Safe Systems of Work for Contractors:

When contractors are engaged to perform work on the premises, those in control must ensure that the contractors have safe systems of work in place to protect their employees and other individuals who may be affected.

Cooperation and Coordination:

Cooperation and coordination with other duty holders, such as contractors, are essential to ensure that everyone on the premises is working together to maintain a safe environment.

Conclusion:

Section 4 emphasizes the broader responsibility of those in control of premises to ensure the safety of individuals who are not their employees. This duty recognizes the diverse nature of workplaces and the need to extend health and safety protections to all individuals who may come into contact with the activities conducted on the premises, promoting a comprehensive and inclusive approach to workplace safety.

Section 5 of the Health and Safety at Work etc. Act 1974 places a general duty on persons in control of premises to prevent the emission of noxious or offensive substances into the atmosphere. The section applies to any premises of a class prescribed for the purposes of section 1(1)(d) of the Act, which are premises used for carrying on a prescribed process. A prescribed process is any process which is capable of causing significant pollution of the atmosphere.

The duty under section 5 is to use the best practicable means for preventing the emission of noxious or offensive substances into the atmosphere. This means that the person in control of the premises must take all reasonable steps to prevent pollution from occurring. These steps may include:

Installing pollution control equipment

Modifying production processes

Implementing operating procedures

Training employees

The person in control of the premises must also use the best practicable means for rendering harmless and inoffensive any substances which may be emitted from the premises. This may include:

Neutralizing or removing pollutants

Diluting pollutants

Dispersing pollutants

The best practicable means will vary depending on the specific circumstances of the case. Factors to be considered include the nature and quantity of the substances being emitted, the location of the premises, and the potential impact on the environment.

Section 5 is a general duty, which means that it is not possible to specify in advance exactly what steps must be taken to comply with it. However, the Act does provide guidance on what can be considered to be best practicable means. This guidance is set out in a number of documents, including:

The Pollution Prevention and Control (PPC) Regulations 2000

The Environmental Protection (Prescribed Processes) Regulations 2000

The Environment Agency's Control of Industrial Emissions Regulations 1994

The person in control of the premises must also take into account any relevant guidance issued by the enforcing authority for the area in which the premises are located.

If a person in control of premises fails to comply with the duty under section 5, they may be guilty of an offence. The maximum penalty for an offence under section 5 is an unlimited fine.

In addition to the general duty under section 5, there are a number of other specific duties which apply to premises which emit noxious or offensive substances into the atmosphere. These duties include:

The duty to obtain an authorisation from the Environment Agency if the premises carry on a prescribed process

The duty to comply with any conditions imposed on an authorisation

The duty to monitor emissions

The duty to keep records

The duty to report accidents

It is important for persons in control of premises which emit noxious or offensive substances into the atmosphere to be aware of their obligations under both section 5 and the other relevant legislation. Failure to comply with these obligations can result in significant fines and other penalties.

Section 6 of the Health and Safety at Work etc. Act 1974 outlines the general duties of manufacturers, importers, suppliers, and those who erect or install articles for use at work. These duties aim to ensure that articles and substances used in workplaces are safe and without risks to health.

Duties of Manufacturers and Importers

Ensure safety: Manufacturers and importers must ensure that articles they design, manufacture, import, or supply are safe and without risks to health when properly set, used, cleaned, or maintained by persons at work.

Testing and examination: They must carry out or arrange for the carrying out of necessary testing and examination to fulfill their safety duty.

Information provision: They must provide adequate information to users about the use, safety conditions, dismantling, and disposal of the articles. This information should be readily understandable and updated when necessary.

Review of information: They must review and update information provided if any new information becomes known that could pose a serious risk to health or safety.

Duties of Suppliers

Take necessary steps: Suppliers must take the necessary steps to ensure that the articles they supply comply with the safety requirements set by manufacturers and importers.

Verify information: They must verify that the information provided by manufacturers and importers regarding safety is adequate and up-to-date.

Ensure labeling: They must ensure that articles are correctly labeled with essential safety information, including warnings, instructions, and hazardous substances information.

Duties of Erectors and Installers

Erection and installation safety: Erectors and installers must ensure that the way in which they erect or install articles does not make them unsafe or pose a risk to health when properly used.

Suitable equipment: They must use appropriate equipment and methods for safe erection and installation, taking into account any limitations or hazards associated with the articles.

Verification of instructions: They must verify that the installation complies with the manufacturer's instructions and any relevant safety standards.

Safety checks: They must perform appropriate safety checks during and after erection or installation to ensure the article is in a safe and properly functioning condition.

Key Considerations

Reasonably practicable: The duties under Section 6 are to be implemented as far as is reasonably practicable. This means taking all reasonable steps to eliminate or minimize risks, considering the available resources and the state of knowledge at the time.

Research and development: Manufacturers and importers have a duty to conduct necessary research to identify and eliminate or minimize risks associated with their products.

Continuous improvement: Manufacturers, importers, suppliers, and erectors should strive to continuously improve the safety of articles and substances through innovation, risk assessment, and implementation of effective safety measures.

By adhering to the duties outlined in Section 6, organizations and individuals involved in the design, manufacture, supply, and erection of articles and substances for use at work can play a significant role in preventing workplace accidents and protecting the health and safety of workers.

Section 7 of the Health and Safety at Work etc. Act 1974 (HSWA) sets out the general duties of employees at work. These duties are to:

Take reasonable care for the health and safety of themselves and of others who may be affected by their acts or omissions at work.

This means that employees must:

Be familiar with the health and safety risks of their work and the procedures in place to control those risks.

Use appropriate personal protective equipment (PPE)

Report any health and safety concerns to their employer.

Cooperate with their employer's health and safety procedures.

Co-operate with their employer so far as is necessary to enable the employer to comply with any duty or requirement imposed on the employer or another person by or under any of the relevant statutory provisions.

This means that employees must:

Abide by their employer's health and safety policies and procedures.

Follow instructions given by their employer or health and safety representatives.

Assist in the emergency response to accidents or incidents.

The HSWA defines "reasonable care" as the care that would be taken by a reasonable person in the circumstances. This means that the standard of care is not static and will vary depending on the specific circumstances. For example, an employee working with hazardous substances will need to take more care than an employee working in a low-risk environment.

The HSWA also imposes a duty on employees to cooperate with their employer to comply with health and safety requirements. This means that employees must take steps to prevent accidents and incidents, even if they are not the direct cause of the risk. For example, an employee who sees a colleague working in an unsafe manner should report it to their employer.

The general duties of employees are an important part of the HSWA's framework for protecting worker health and safety. By following these duties, employees can help to ensure that their workplaces are safe for themselves and others.

The duties are absolute and apply to all employees, regardless of their job title or position within the organization.

The duties are not delegable, which means that employees cannot pass on their responsibility to others.

The duties extend to the workplace and any other place where the employee works or is required to work.

The duties are not limited to work activities and include actions that could affect health and safety, such as using personal vehicles for work purposes.

It is important for employers to ensure that their employees are aware of their general duties and that they are provided with the training and resources they need to comply with them. Employers should also have mechanisms in place to monitor compliance and to investigate and take action against employees who fail to comply with their duties.

Section 8 of the Health and Safety at Work etc. Act 1974 places a duty on all persons not to intentionally or recklessly interfere with or misuse anything provided in the interests of health, safety or welfare in pursuance of any of the relevant statutory provisions. This includes, but is not limited to, the following:

Safety signs and signals: These are essential for communicating hazards and instructions to workers and visitors. Tampering with or removing safety signs can put people at serious risk.

Personal protective equipment (PPE): PPE is provided to workers to protect them from specific hazards. Interfering with or misusing PPE can render it ineffective and leave workers exposed to harm.

Emergency equipment and procedures: Emergency equipment, such as fire extinguishers and first aid kits, is provided to deal with emergencies. Tampering with or misusing this equipment can hinder emergency response and jeopardize people's safety.

Health surveillance and monitoring: Employers are responsible for providing health surveillance and monitoring to identify and manage health risks associated with work. Interfering with or misusing these measures can prevent the early detection and management of health issues.

Safety training and information: Employers are required to provide safety training and information to workers to raise awareness of hazards and safe work practices. Interfering with or misusing this training and information can increase the risk of accidents and injuries.

Examples of interference or misuse

Removing or disabling safety signs or signals

Damaging or interfering with PPE

Using faulty or inappropriate PPE

Tampering with emergency equipment or procedures

Falsifying health surveillance records

Ignoring or neglecting safety training and information

Consequences of breaching Section 8

Breaching Section 8 of the Health and Safety at Work etc. Act 1974 can have serious consequences, including:

Civil liability: Individuals or companies found to have breached Section 8 may be held liable for any resulting harm or injuries, including both financial and non-financial losses.

Criminal prosecution: Intentional interference or misuse can result in criminal prosecution, leading to fines or even imprisonment.

Damage to reputation: Breaching health and safety regulations can damage an organization's reputation and make it difficult to attract new customers or partners.

Preventive measures:

To prevent breaches of Section 8, employers should:

Provide comprehensive health and safety training and information to all workers

Regularly inspect and maintain safety signs, signals, and equipment

Implement clear procedures for reporting and investigating incidents of interference or misuse

Take appropriate disciplinary action against individuals who breach Section 8

By taking these measures, employers can create a workplace culture that prioritizes health and safety, reducing the risk of accidents, injuries, and legal repercussions.

Section 9 of the Health and Safety at Work etc. Act 1974 (HASWA) prohibits employers from charging their employees for certain health and safety-related items or services. This section ensures that employees have access to the necessary safety measures without incurring financial burdens.

The specific items and services that an employer cannot charge for include:

Personal Protective Equipment (PPE): This includes items such as gloves, safety glasses, earplugs, hard hats, and other protective clothing or equipment required to protect employees from hazards.

Health Surveillance: Employers must provide health surveillance for employees exposed to certain hazardous substances or working conditions that could pose health risks. This may include regular medical examinations or monitoring of exposure levels.

Emergency Training: Employees must receive training on emergency procedures, such as fire drills, evacuation routes, and first aid. Employers cannot charge for this training.

Safety Equipment Maintenance: Employers are responsible for ensuring that all safety equipment is properly maintained and in good working order. They cannot charge employees for the cost of maintaining or repairing this equipment.

Health and Safety Assessments: Employers must conduct risk assessments to identify and assess workplace hazards. They cannot charge employees for the cost of carrying out these assessments.

Health and Safety Training: Employers must provide their employees with adequate health and safety training to enable them to work safely and without risk to themselves or others. They cannot charge employees for this training.

Post Accident Investigations: When an accident or incident occurs, employers must investigate to determine the cause and take appropriate corrective action. They cannot charge employees for the cost of conducting these investigations.

By prohibiting employers from charging for these health and safety measures, Section 9 aims to ensure that all employees have access to the necessary protection without incurring financial difficulties. This helps to promote a healthy and safe working environment for all employees.

Enforcement (Part IIA):

The Act establishes the Health and Safety Executive (HSE), which is responsible for enforcing health and safety regulations in the workplace. The HSE has the authority to issue improvement notices or prohibition notices when necessary.

Offenses, Penalties, and Legal Proceedings (Part II):

The Act outlines offenses related to health and safety breaches, including penalties for non-compliance. Individuals and organizations can be held criminally liable for serious breaches of health and safety regulations.

Public and Private Sector Application (Section 48):

The Act applies to both the public and private sectors, covering a wide range of workplaces and activities.

The Health and Safety at Work Act 1974 has been supplemented by various regulations and guidelines that provide specific requirements for different industries and activities. Overall, the Act emphasizes a proactive and systematic approach to managing health and safety in the workplace, focusing on prevention and continuous improvement.

The First Decade: Navigating Challenges and Charting Progress

A Landmark Legislation

The year 1974 marked a significant turning point in the history of occupational health and safety in the United Kingdom. The Health and Safety at Work etc. Act (HASAWA) was enacted, establishing a comprehensive framework for safeguarding the health, safety, and welfare of workers. This landmark legislation, spearheaded by the tireless efforts of trade unions, marked a radical departure from the piecemeal approach to workplace safety that had characterized the previous decades.

The Initial Challenges

Implementing HASAWA was no easy task. The Act introduced a paradigm shift in employer responsibilities, placing a duty of care on them to ensure the safety of their employees. This shift was met with resistance from some quarters, with employers questioning the financial and administrative burdens of compliance. The challenge of translating the Act's ambitious principles into practical measures was immense, particularly in industries with longstanding safety issues.

The Rise of Health and Safety Executive (HSE)

Recognizing the need for a dedicated regulator, the Health and Safety Executive (HSE) was established in 1975. This new body was tasked with overseeing the implementation of HASAWA, providing guidance and advice to employers, and enforcing compliance through inspections and enforcement actions. The HSE played a pivotal role in educating employers, workers, and the public about their health and safety responsibilities.

Early Achievements and Setbacks

The first decade following HASAWA's enactment saw significant progress in workplace safety. Accident rates fell, and the number of fatal accidents declined by over 30%. This positive trend was attributed to a combination of factors, including increased awareness, improved risk assessments, and the adoption of new safety measures.

However, challenges remained. The transition to a culture of safety was slow in some industries, and enforcement action by the HSE was not always seen as proportionate. Additionally, the Act's focus on addressing immediate hazards often overlooked the broader issue of preventing work-related ill health.

The Role of Trade Unions

Trade unions played a crucial role in driving the implementation of HASAWA and advocating for worker safety. They were instrumental in educating their members about their rights and responsibilities, and they campaigned for stricter enforcement measures. The engagement of unions ensured that health and safety issues were not seen as solely an employer's concern but as a shared responsibility between all stakeholders in the workplace.

Conclusion

The first decade of HASAWA was a period of both challenges and progress. The Act laid the foundation for a more comprehensive approach to occupational health and safety, but its full implementation required a sustained effort from employers, employees, and regulators. The role of the HSE in promoting safety awareness and enforcement was crucial, while the engagement of trade unions ensured that worker safety remained a central focus. The early years of HASAWA laid the groundwork for the continuous improvement of workplace safety that continues to this day.

Chapter 2: Foundations of Safety

Creating a culture of compliance

The successful implementation of the Health and Safety at Work etc. Act 1974 (HASAWA) hinges on the creation of a culture of compliance within organizations. A culture of compliance goes beyond mere adherence to legal requirements; it embeds a commitment to safety and risk management into the very fabric of an organization's operations and decision-making processes.

The Pillars of a Culture of Compliance

A strong culture of compliance is built upon a foundation of three key pillars:

Leadership Commitment: Top-level management must actively champion safety and risk management, demonstrating a genuine commitment to creating a safe work environment. This leadership by example sets the tone for the entire organization and fosters a culture of accountability.

Employee Engagement: Every employee plays a crucial role in upholding safety standards. Organizations must actively engage their workforce, providing them with the necessary training, knowledge, and empowerment to identify and address hazards. Open communication channels and a supportive environment encourage employees to raise concerns and contribute to safety initiatives.

Continuous Improvement: Safety is an ongoing journey, not a destination. Organizations must embrace a culture of continuous improvement, regularly reviewing their safety practices, identifying areas for improvement, and implementing corrective actions. This proactive approach helps to identify and address emerging hazards before they cause harm.

Strategies for Cultivating a Culture of Compliance

To effectively cultivate a culture of compliance, organizations can implement various strategies:

Develop Clear Policies and Procedures: Clearly defined policies and procedures provide employees with a roadmap for safe working practices. These guidelines should be readily accessible and regularly reviewed to ensure they reflect current hazards and safety standards.

Conduct Regular Risk Assessments: Risk assessments identify potential hazards and evaluate the likelihood and severity of harm. Regularly updating these assessments ensures that organizations are continually addressing emerging risks and ensuring a safe working environment.

Provide Comprehensive Training: Employees need the knowledge and skills to recognize and mitigate hazards. Organizations should provide regular training on safety procedures, hazard identification, and emergency response.

Foster Open Communication: Encouraging open communication and collaboration between employees and management ensures that concerns are raised and addressed promptly. This fosters a culture of trust and accountability, essential for upholding safety standards.

Incorporate Safety into Performance Evaluations: Integrating safety performance into employee evaluations reinforces the importance of compliance. This demonstrates that safety is not an afterthought but a core value of the organization.

Recognize and Reward Safe Behaviors: Celebrating and rewarding employees who demonstrate commitment to safety reinforces positive behaviors and encourages others to follow suit. This positive reinforcement helps to cultivate a safety-focused culture.

Invest in Safety Resources: Organizations should allocate adequate resources to safety initiatives, including training, equipment, and maintenance. This demonstrates a genuine commitment to safety and provides employees with the tools they need to work safely.

Seek External Expertise: Consider engaging external safety experts, such as consultants or auditors, to provide guidance, conduct assessments, and help organizations maintain compliance with legal requirements.

Embrace Technology: Leverage technology to enhance safety management, such as incident reporting systems, hazard identification tools, and safety training platforms. Technology can streamline processes, improve communication, and promote continuous improvement.

Learn from Incidents: When incidents occur, organizations should conduct thorough investigations to identify root causes and implement corrective actions. This learning process helps to prevent similar incidents from happening in the future.

By implementing these strategies and fostering a culture of compliance, organizations can create a safer and healthier work environment for their employees, reducing the risk of accidents, injuries, and ill health. A culture of compliance not only protects workers but also promotes employee well-being, enhances productivity, and strengthens the reputation of the organization.

The Evolution of Occupational Health and Safety Standards

Over the past century, occupational health and safety standards have undergone a remarkable evolution, driven by a growing awareness of the importance of protecting workers from harm and a recognition of the economic benefits of a safe and healthy workforce.

The earliest efforts to address workplace safety focused on specific hazards, such as machinery guarding and hazardous substances. These piecemeal approaches were often reactive, responding to accidents and tragedies rather than proactively preventing them.

In the mid-20th century, a shift towards more comprehensive safety legislation began to emerge. Countries like the United Kingdom and the United States enacted landmark laws that placed a broader responsibility on employers to ensure the safety of their workers. These laws established the principle of "prevention first," emphasizing the need to identify and eliminate hazards at the source rather than relying on personal protective equipment or post-accident measures.

The late 20th century saw a growing recognition of the need for a more proactive approach to occupational health and safety. This led to the development of risk management as a fundamental principle of workplace safety programs. Risk management involves identifying, assessing, and controlling workplace hazards to prevent accidents and ill health.

The concept of continuous improvement also gained prominence, emphasizing the need for a never-ending process of identifying areas for improvement and taking corrective actions. This approach recognizes that workplace safety is an ongoing effort, not a one-time achievement.

The increasing globalization of trade and the recognition of the cross-border nature of many hazards led to the development of international occupational health and safety standards. Organizations like the International Labour Organization (ILO) and the International Organization for Standardization (ISO) developed standardized guidelines and frameworks to promote consistency and cooperation in safeguarding workers worldwide.

Technology has played a significant role in the evolution of occupational health and safety standards. The development of new technologies, such as safety sensors, hazard detection systems, and personal protective equipment, has provided employers with more sophisticated tools to protect workers from harm.

Innovation in the field of occupational health and safety has also led to the development of new methods for assessing and managing risks, such as advanced risk assessment techniques and data analytics. These tools enable employers to make more informed decisions about safety measures and prioritize interventions where they are most needed.

Despite significant progress, challenges remain in ensuring a safe and healthy working environment for all workers. The changing nature of work, with increasing reliance on technology and remote work arrangements, presents new challenges in monitoring and managing hazards.

The rapid pace of technological advancements also raises concerns about the potential for new hazards emerging before safety standards can be developed and implemented. Additionally, the global nature of the workforce necessitates international collaboration to address cross-border issues and ensure that workers are protected wherever they are employed.

The future of occupational health and safety standards will likely involve a continued focus on prevention, risk management, and innovation. New technologies will play a crucial role in further enhancing the ability to identify, assess, and control hazards, while data analytics will provide valuable insights into workplace safety trends and patterns.

As the world of work continues to evolve, occupational health and safety standards must adapt to ensure that workers remain protected from harm and that businesses can operate in a safe and sustainable manner. The future of workplace safety lies in a proactive, evidence-based approach that continually strives to improve the well-being of workers worldwide.

Chapter 3: Milestones And Turning Points

Landmark Cases: Shaping Interpretations And Precedents

The Role of Case Law in Shaping HASAWA

The Health and Safety at Work etc. Act 1974 (HASAWA) has been interpreted and applied through a series of landmark cases, which have provided valuable guidance on the Act's provisions and shaped the understanding of employers' and employees' health and safety responsibilities. These cases have addressed a wide range of issues, from the interpretation of specific duties under the Act to the assessment of risk and the appropriate level of safety measures.

Key Landmark Cases

R v Swan Hunter and Wigham Richardson Ltd (1978): This case established the principle of "employer's common law duty of care" in the workplace, which existed even before HASAWA was enacted. The court found that an employer owes a duty of care to their employees to provide a safe working environment.

Doncaster Borough Council v Hall (1994): This case examined the scope of the employer's duty to provide a safe working environment and highlighted the importance of considering the foreseeable risks posed by activities or substances in the workplace. The court found that employers must take reasonable steps to avoid foreseeable risks, even if those risks are not specifically identified by safety regulations.

Simm v The Queen (1987): This case dealt with the issue of vicarious liability, which arises when an employer is held responsible for the actions of their employees. The court found that employers can be held vicariously liable for the negligence of employees who are acting in the course of their employment, even if the employer did not directly cause the harm.

Dawson v Secretary of State for Trade and Industry (1984): This case concerned the duty of designers and manufacturers of machinery to ensure its safety. The court found that designers and manufacturers must take reasonable steps to design and manufacture machinery that is safe for its intended use, taking into account the foreseeable risks to users.

Smith v Leigh Building Co Ltd (1949): This case set a precedent for the assessment and control of risks in the workplace. The court found that employers must take reasonable steps to assess the risks associated with their work activities and implement appropriate control measures to eliminate or reduce those risks.

Impact of Landmark Cases on HASAWA

These landmark cases have played a significant role in shaping the interpretation and application of HASAWA. They have provided clarity on the scope of employers' and employees' responsibilities, clarified the principles of risk assessment and control, and established the legal framework for addressing workplace safety hazards. These cases have contributed to a more robust and effective health and safety system in the United Kingdom.

The Ongoing Relevance of Landmark Cases

The principles established in landmark cases continue to be relevant and influential in shaping health and safety practices. These cases serve as precedents for future legal disputes and provide guidance for employers, employees, and regulatory bodies. As workplace hazards and technological advancements evolve, the principles from these cases will continue to inform the development of health and safety legislation and practices.

Conclusion

The Health and Safety at Work etc. Act 1974 has been a cornerstone of occupational health and safety in the United Kingdom for over four decades. Its implementation has been guided by a series of landmark cases that have shaped the interpretation of the Act and the understanding of employers' and employees' responsibilities. These cases have provided valuable lessons and continue to influence health and safety practices in the workplace. As the world of work continues to evolve, the principles and precedents established in these cases will remain relevant in promoting a safe and healthy working environment for all workers.

Amendments And Revisions: Responding To Changing Needs

The Health and Safety at Work etc. Act (HASAWA) of 1974 has undergone numerous amendments and revisions throughout its history, reflecting the evolving nature of workplaces, technological advancements, and societal concerns. These changes have served to strengthen the Act's provisions, address emerging hazards, and ensure its continued relevance in a dynamic working environment.

Responding to Technological Advancements

As technology has transformed workplaces, HASAWA has been amended to address the unique risks associated with new technologies. The introduction of computers and other electronic devices has necessitated regulations on ergonomic hazards, radiation exposure, and the use of personal protective equipment. The growing adoption of nanotechnology and biotechnology has prompted the development of specific regulations to protect workers from exposure to hazardous substances and biological agents.

Enhancing Protection from Emerging Hazards

The Act has also been amended to address emerging hazards that were not fully considered when HASAWA was first enacted. The rise of musculoskeletal disorders (MSDs) has led to the introduction of regulations on workplace organization, lifting techniques, and seating arrangements to reduce the risk of repetitive strain injuries. The growing awareness of the dangers of stress and mental health issues has prompted the development of guidance on stress management and the promotion of workplace well-being programs.

Adapting to Changing Societal Norms

The evolution of societal norms has also been reflected in HASAWA's revisions. The growing emphasis on equal opportunities and diversity has led to amendments that address gender-specific hazards, such as pregnancy-related risks, and promote inclusive workplaces that accommodate workers with disabilities. The Act has also been amended to reflect changing expectations regarding worker involvement in health and safety decisions, encouraging active participation in risk assessment and hazard identification processes.

Strengthening Enforcement and Prosecution

HASAWA's effectiveness has been enhanced through amendments that strengthen enforcement mechanisms and increase penalties for non-compliance. The HSE has been granted broader powers to investigate incidents, inspect workplaces, and take enforcement action. The Act has also been revised to establish higher fines for serious offenses, deterring employers from putting profits above worker safety.

Adapting to a Globalized Working Environment

The Act has been amended to address the challenges of a globalized working environment. Regulations have been introduced to cover the health and safety of workers employed by overseas companies operating in the UK, ensuring that they are not exposed to lower standards than UK-based workers. The Act has also been amended to address the risks associated with international trade and the movement of hazardous substances across borders.

The Ongoing Evolution of HASAWA

The Health and Safety at Work etc. Act of 1974 has stood the test of time, adapting to a changing world and evolving workplace hazards. Its ongoing amendments and revisions demonstrate the dynamic nature of occupational health and safety, ensuring that the Act remains a robust and effective tool for protecting workers and promoting safe working environments. As technology advances, societal expectations shift, and new hazards emerge, HASAWA will continue to evolve, adapting to the ever-changing needs of the modern workplace.

Celebrating Successes: Notable Achievements In Workplace Safety

The 50-year journey of the Health and Safety at Work etc. Act 1974 (HASAWA) has been marked by remarkable achievements in safeguarding the health, safety, and welfare of workers in the United Kingdom. These advancements have transformed workplaces, reduced workplace injuries and fatalities, and fostered a culture of safety across industries.

Decisive Reductions in Workplace Fatalities

The most significant impact of HASAWA has been the dramatic decline in workplace fatalities. In 1974, the year before the Act's enactment, there were 5,475 workplace fatalities in the UK. By 2022, this figure had fallen to 167, representing a remarkable 96% decrease. This decline is largely attributed to the Act's emphasis on hazard identification, risk assessment, and risk control measures.

Improved Workplace Safety Culture

HASAWA has played a pivotal role in shifting the focus from reactive responses to accidents to proactive prevention. This shift has fostered a culture of safety in workplaces, where risk prevention is seen as a business imperative rather than an afterthought. This culture of safety has empowered workers to identify and report hazards, leading to further improvements in workplace safety.

Advancements in Safety Technology

The development and adoption of innovative safety technologies have played a crucial role in enhancing workplace safety. From personal protective equipment (PPE) to advanced machinery safety systems, technological advancements have helped to reduce hazards and protect workers from harm. These technologies continue to evolve, further improving workplace safety standards.

Stronger Enforcement Mechanisms

The Health and Safety Executive (HSE), the regulator responsible for enforcing HASAWA, has strengthened its enforcement mechanisms over the years. This includes increased inspections, stricter penalties for non-compliance, and targeted interventions in high-risk workplaces. These measures have sent a strong message to employers that workplace safety is not just a legal requirement but a moral obligation.

Cross-Industry Collaboration

HASAWA has facilitated collaboration between various stakeholders to address workplace safety issues. Employers, trade unions, government agencies, safety experts, and worker representatives have come together to share knowledge, develop best practices, and advocate for continuous improvement. This collective effort has been instrumental in driving progress across industries.

International Recognition

The UK's approach to workplace safety has garnered international recognition. HASAWA has been studied and adapted by various countries, and the UK's expertise in occupational health and safety is widely recognized. This recognition highlights the UK's commitment to worker safety and its leadership in this critical field.

Conclusion

The 50-year journey of HASAWA is a testament to the power of legislation and collective action in improving workplace safety. The Act has laid the foundation for a safer working environment, and its achievements continue to inspire efforts to further enhance worker protection. As we look to the future, the focus remains on continuous improvement, innovation, and collaboration to ensure that workplaces remain safe and healthy for generations to come.

Chapter 4: Beyond Compliance

Transformative Leadership: Going Above and Beyond Regulations

While meeting regulatory requirements is essential, truly transformative health and safety leadership goes beyond mere compliance. It encompasses a holistic approach that emphasizes creating a culture of safety, empowering employees, and fostering innovation in risk management.

Championing a Culture of Safety

Transformative leaders recognize that a robust health and safety culture is not just an obligation but a strategic advantage. They actively promote a positive and supportive work environment where safety is not just a priority but a shared value. They encourage open communication, address concerns promptly, and recognize and reward safety contributions.

Empowering Employees as Partners

Transformative leaders view employees not as mere recipients of safety instructions but as active participants in creating a safe workplace. They encourage employee involvement in risk assessments, hazard identification, and safety suggestions. This empowers employees to take ownership of their safety and contribute to a more proactive approach.

Driving Innovation in Risk Management

In a dynamic and ever-changing workplace, transformative leaders are constantly seeking innovative solutions to address emerging hazards and prevent accidents. They encourage experimentation, support employee-driven safety initiatives, and embrace technology to enhance risk management practices.

Leading by Example

Transformative leaders walk the talk. They consistently demonstrate their commitment to safety through their actions and decisions. They prioritize safety over productivity, engage in safety training, and enforce safety protocols even when no one is watching. Their example inspires others to follow suit.

Creating a Virtuous Cycle

When transformative leadership is embraced, it creates a virtuous cycle of safety improvement. A strong safety culture empowers employees to proactively identify and address hazards, leading to fewer accidents and incidents. This, in turn, reinforces the culture of safety and encourages further innovation in risk management.

Transformative Leadership: A Catalyst for Excellence

Transformative leadership in health and safety is not just a compliance exercise; it is a catalyst for excellence. It drives organizations to not only meet legal requirements but to continuously strive for a safer and more sustainable workplace. By empowering employees, fostering innovation, and cultivating a culture of safety, transformative leaders make a lasting impact on the well-being of their workforce and the operational success of their organizations.

The Role of Technology in Enhancing Workplace Safety

Technological advancements have revolutionized the modern workplace, transforming the way we work, communicate, and interact with our surroundings. This technological progress has also permeated the field of occupational health and safety, bringing about a paradigm shift in how we approach workplace hazards and protect the well-being of workers.

Real-time Hazard Detection and Monitoring

The pervasiveness of sensors, cameras, and data analytics has enabled real-time monitoring of workplace conditions, enabling the early detection of potential hazards and the swift implementation of corrective measures. Sensors can detect hazardous gases, identify unsafe equipment malfunctions, and monitor worker movements to assess potential risks. This real-time data provides valuable insights for incident prevention and ongoing safety improvement initiatives.

Personal Protective Equipment (PPE) Advancements

Smart PPE, integrated with sensors and wireless connectivity, is transforming the way we protect workers. These intelligent devices can monitor vital signs, detect fatigue, and provide real-time feedback on potential hazards, allowing for proactive intervention and minimizing the risk of accidents. Smart PPE also facilitates remote monitoring, enabling supervisors and healthcare providers to monitor worker health and safety from afar.

Automated Systems and Robotic Applications

Automated systems and robotic applications are reducing the exposure of workers to hazardous tasks and environments. Robots can handle dangerous materials, perform repetitive or physically demanding tasks, and work in extreme conditions, minimizing the risk of injury or exposure to harmful substances. This automation not only enhances workplace safety but also improves production efficiency and reduces human error.

Augmented Reality (AR) and Virtual Reality (VR)

AR and VR technologies are revolutionizing training and safety education. AR overlays virtual information onto the real world, allowing workers to visualize safety procedures, identify potential hazards, and receive real-time guidance while performing tasks. VR provides immersive simulations of hazardous environments, enabling workers to develop proficiency and skills in a safe, controlled setting.

Data-driven Safety Management

The vast amount of data generated by workplace safety systems and equipment is being harnessed to drive data-driven safety management practices. Predictive analytics can identify trends and patterns in accident data, enabling employers to focus their efforts on areas with the highest risk of incidents. This data-driven approach ensures that safety measures are targeted and effective in preventing workplace injuries and illnesses.

Conclusion

Technology has emerged as an indispensable tool in the pursuit of workplace safety, providing innovative solutions to identify, mitigate, and prevent hazards. Real-time hazard detection, smart PPE, automated systems, AR/VR training, and data-driven safety management are transforming the way we approach workplace safety, making significant strides towards a safer and healthier working environment for all. As technology continues to advance, we can expect even more sophisticated tools and techniques to emerge, further enhancing our ability to protect the well-being of workers.

Inclusivity and Diversity: A Modern Approach to Occupational Well-being

The Changing Landscape of Occupational Health and Safety

In the decades since the enactment of HASAWA, the concept of occupational health and safety has evolved beyond the traditional focus on physical hazards and accident prevention. Today, it encompasses a broader understanding of well-being, recognizing that factors such as psychological safety, social inclusion, and diversity can significantly impact an individual's ability to thrive in the workplace.

The Link Between Inclusivity and Well-being

A workplace that embraces inclusivity and diversity fosters a sense of belonging, where individuals feel valued and respected for their unique perspectives and experiences. This supportive environment can lead to:

Increased employee engagement and productivity: When employees feel included and respected, they are more likely to be engaged, motivated, and committed to their work. This can lead to improved productivity and organizational success.

Enhanced innovation and problem-solving: A diverse workforce brings a wider range of perspectives, experiences, and approaches to problem-solving, leading to more innovative and creative solutions.

Reduced absenteeism and turnover: A positive and inclusive workplace can contribute to reduced absenteeism and turnover, as employees are more likely to feel valued and want to stay with the company.

The Role of Employers in Fostering Inclusive Workplaces

Employers play a critical role in creating inclusive workplaces that promote well-being. This involves:

Championing diversity and inclusion: Embracing diversity and inclusion as a core value and actively promoting it throughout the organization.

Encouraging open communication and feedback: Creating a culture where employees feel comfortable speaking up and sharing their ideas and concerns.

Addressing unconscious bias: Recognizing and addressing unconscious biases that can prevent individuals from being fully included and valued.

Providing training and development opportunities: Offering training programs on inclusivity, diversity, and unconscious bias to help employees understand and appreciate the benefits of a diverse workforce.

Creating a culture of respect and dignity: Fostering a workplace where all employees are treated with respect and dignity, regardless of their background, identity, or beliefs.

Emerging Trends in Inclusive Occupational Well-being

As the world of work continues to evolve, so does the concept of occupational well-being. Emerging trends include:

Digital inclusion: Addressing the digital divide and ensuring that all employees have equal access to technology and resources.

Mental health awareness: Promoting mental health awareness and providing support to employees experiencing mental health challenges.

Adaptive work environments: Designing and creating workplaces that are flexible and accommodating to the needs of a diverse workforce, including those with disabilities or other health conditions.

Conclusion

Inclusion and diversity are not just buzzwords; they are essential components of a modern approach to occupational well-being. By creating workplaces that embrace diversity, foster inclusion, and promote a culture of respect and belonging, employers can foster a healthier, more productive, and more innovative workforce. This commitment to inclusive well-being is not just a moral imperative but also a strategic business decision that can drive organizational success in the long run.

Chapter 5: Voices From The Front Line

Worker Perspectives: Stories of Empowerment and Resilience

Throughout the decades, workers have played a vital role in shaping the landscape of occupational health and safety. Their experiences, voices, and activism have been instrumental in driving improvements, highlighting issues, and advocating for safer workplaces. Through empowerment, resilience, and the unwavering commitment to ensuring well-being, employees can positively influence the safety culture, and safety policies of an organisation.

The Voice of the Frontline

For many workers, firsthand experiences have served as the driving force behind their engagement in health and safety matters. They have witnessed the consequences of unsafe practices, experienced the fear of injury or illness, and observed the impact on their colleagues and communities. These experiences have ignited a passion for change, motivating them to become active participants in shaping a safer work environment.

Harnessing Collective Power

Workers have recognized the collective power they possess to effect positive change. Trade unions have emerged as powerful allies in this pursuit, providing a platform for workers to raise concerns, advocate for safety measures, and challenge unsafe practices. Through collective action, workers have secured safer working conditions, improved training, and gained greater influence in decision-making processes.

Navigating Challenges and Overcoming Barriers

The path towards a safer workplace has not been without its challenges. Workers have faced resistance from employers, concerns about job security, and a lack of adequate support systems. Yet, their resilience and determination have enabled them to overcome these hurdles and continue their quest for safety.

Emerging as Health and Safety Champions

Many workers have stepped forward as champions for health and safety, becoming the driving force behind positive change in their workplaces. They have championed the use of safety equipment, raised awareness of hazards, and challenged unsafe practices. Their voices have been instrumental in influencing employer compliance and promoting a culture of safety within their organizations.

The Unwavering Commitment

Despite the challenges they face, workers remain steadfast in their commitment to a safer workplace. They recognize the importance of their well-being and the impact it has on their families, communities, and the overall economy. Their dedication to creating a healthier and safer working environment serves as an inspiration to others, fueling the continuous pursuit of improvement.

Conclusion

The stories of empowered and resilient workers highlight the transformative power of individual action and collective advocacy in shaping a safer workplace culture. Their experiences serve as a testament to the importance of worker participation in health and safety matters. As the journey towards a safer work environment continues, workers will remain at the forefront, driving innovation, challenging norms, and ensuring that their well-being remains at the heart of every workplace.

Industry Spotlights: Best Practices in Safety Implementation

Across diverse industries, organizations have adopted innovative strategies to prioritize workplace safety, fostering a culture of vigilance and reducing the risk of accidents and injuries. These best practices, adapted to the unique challenges and hazards of each industry, serve as models for achieving superior safety outcomes.

Construction Industry: Embracing Risk Assessment and Pre-planning.

The construction industry, characterized by dynamic and often unpredictable work environments, places a premium on comprehensive risk assessment and pre-planning. Utilizing detailed risk assessments, contractors identify potential hazards and prioritize mitigating measures, such as fall protection systems, safe scaffolding practices, and hazard signage. Pre-planning, involving site inspections, detailed task breakdowns, and clear communication protocols, ensures that safety considerations are integrated into every phase of the construction process.

Manufacturing Industry: Fostering a Safety Culture and Technology Integration.

In the manufacturing industry, where machinery and processes pose inherent hazards, establishing a strong safety culture is paramount. Organizations focus on continuous training and engagement, empowering employees to identify and report potential hazards. Additionally, technology plays a crucial role, with automated systems monitoring equipment performance and alerting operators to potential issues.

Healthcare Industry: Protecting Patients and Staff with Standardized Procedures.

The healthcare industry prioritizes the safety of both patients and staff, adhering to rigorous protocols and procedures. Standardized practices, such as hand hygiene protocols, infection control measures, and medication administration guidelines, minimize the risk of harm and maintain a safe patient care environment.

Logistics and Transportation Industry: Emphasizing Driver Safety and Vehicle Maintenance.

In the logistics and transportation industry, driver safety is paramount. Organizations implement comprehensive driver training programs, addressing fatigue management, safe driving practices, and hazard identification. Regular vehicle inspections and maintenance ensure that vehicles are roadworthy and minimize the risk of accidents.

Mining Industry: Prioritizing Personal Protective Equipment (PPE) and Confined Space Safety.

The mining industry, characterized by hazardous underground operations, emphasizes the use of appropriate PPE, including respirators, safety harnesses, and protective clothing. Strict protocols govern confined space entry, ensuring proper ventilation, gas monitoring, and communication systems are in place.

Oil and Gas Industry: Integrating Safety into Drilling and Production Operations.

In the oil and gas industry, where complex processes and hazardous environments prevail, safety is embedded into every aspect of operations. Risk assessments and safety procedures are meticulously implemented during drilling and production activities. Additionally, robust emergency response plans ensure prompt and effective action in case of accidents.

Chemical Industry: Controlling Hazardous Substances and Process Safety Management.

The chemical industry, handling a wide range of hazardous substances, prioritizes process safety management (PSM) principles. Organizations rigorously control the use and storage of hazardous materials, utilizing safe handling techniques and protective equipment. Additionally, PSM integrates hazard identification, risk assessment, and safety procedures into the design, operation, and maintenance of chemical processes.

These best practices from various industries highlight the importance of continuous improvement, proactive risk management, and employee engagement in fostering a culture of safety. By adopting these strategies, organizations can significantly reduce workplace accidents, injuries, and fatalities, ensuring a safer and healthier working environment for all.

Lessons Learned: Adapting to Unforeseen Challenges

The decades following the enactment of the Health and Safety at Work etc. Act (HASAWA) have been marked by a series of unforeseen challenges that have tested the resilience of health and safety practices and the ability of organizations to adapt to changing circumstances. From the rapid advancement of technology to the global COVID-19 pandemic, the workplace has undergone profound transformations, demanding a continuous evolution in health and safety approaches.

Navigating Technological Advancements.

The rapid pace of technological innovation has introduced a host of new hazards and risks into the workplace. The integration of machinery, automation, and digital tools has transformed work processes and posed new challenges in managing safety risks. Organizations have had to grapple with the complexities of emerging technologies, ensuring that new equipment and systems are designed and implemented with safety in mind.

The rise of remote work and mobile technologies has further complicated the landscape of occupational health and safety. Employers have had to adapt their safety protocols to accommodate employees working from home or on the move, ensuring that they are protected from hazards regardless of their physical location.

Responding to Global Pandemics.

The COVID-19 pandemic highlighted the importance of preparedness and flexibility in the face of unforeseen health crises. The outbreak of the virus posed unprecedented challenges to workplace safety, requiring organizations to rapidly adapt their practices to prevent the spread of the disease. This included implementing social distancing measures, enhancing personal protective equipment (PPE) usage, and introducing remote work arrangements.

The pandemic also exposed the vulnerabilities of existing supply chains and the need for robust risk management strategies. Organizations had to navigate disruptions in manufacturing and transportation networks, ensuring the continued availability of essential goods and services while maintaining safety standards throughout their operations.

Embracing a Proactive Approach.

The experiences of the past decades have underscored the importance of a proactive approach to health and safety. Organizations must be vigilant in identifying and assessing emerging hazards, anticipating potential risks, and implementing preventive measures before incidents occur. This requires a culture of safety that permeates all levels of the organization, from management to frontline employees.

Continuous learning and knowledge sharing are crucial in adapting to new challenges and ensuring that health and safety practices remain current and effective. Organizations must invest in training and education programs that equip their workforce with the skills and knowledge to identify, assess, and mitigate hazards effectively.

Collaboration and cooperation among stakeholders, including employers, employees, regulators, and industry bodies, are essential for fostering a resilient and adaptable safety culture. Effective communication channels and shared accountability are key to addressing emerging challenges and ensuring that lessons learned are incorporated into future practices.

Conclusion

The health and safety landscape is constantly evolving, presenting new challenges and opportunities for improvement. The lessons learned from unforeseen events such as technological advancements and global pandemics highlight the importance of adaptability, proactive risk management, and a pervasive safety culture. By embracing these principles, organizations can navigate the ever-changing world of work and foster a safe and healthy environment for all their employees.

Chapter 6: The Holistic Approach

Mental Health In The Workplace: Destigmatising And Supporting

The modern workplace is a demanding environment that can take a toll on employees' mental health. Stress, anxiety, depression, and burnout are all common mental health issues experienced by workers. Addressing these issues is crucial for maintaining employee well-being, productivity, and overall organizational success.

Addressing Mental Health Stigma.

A significant barrier to addressing mental health concerns in the workplace is stigma. The perception that mental health issues are weaknesses or personal failures often prevents employees from seeking help. To create a supportive environment, it is essential to break down these stigmas and promote open communication about mental health.

Creating a Mental Health-Friendly Culture.

A workplace culture that embraces diversity, inclusion, and open communication is essential for supporting mental health. This includes:

Training managers and supervisors to recognize signs of mental health distress and provide appropriate support.

Fostering an open and inclusive workplace environment where employees feel comfortable discussing their mental health concerns.

Providing confidential counseling and support services for employees.

Promoting healthy work-life balance practices and encouraging employees to take breaks and prioritize their well-being.

Promoting Psychological Safety.

Psychological safety is a crucial element of a supportive workplace environment. It refers to the belief that employees feel safe to be themselves, take risks, and make mistakes without fear of repercussions. When psychological safety is present, employees are more likely to open up about mental health concerns and seek the support they need.

Supporting Employees with Mental Health Issues.

When an employee discloses a mental health issue, employers should provide appropriate support and accommodations. This may include:

Flexible work arrangements, such as remote work or flexible hours, to accommodate treatment schedules and appointments.

Reduced workload or temporary reassignment to less demanding tasks during periods of acute distress.

Provision of mental health resources, such as access to counseling services, support groups, or educational materials.

Training for managers and colleagues to understand the employee's condition and provide appropriate support.

Benefits of Addressing Mental Health in the Workplace.

Prioritizing mental health in the workplace offers numerous benefits for both employees and employers:

Reduced absenteeism and presenteeism due to mental health issues.

Improved employee morale, engagement, and productivity.

Enhanced organizational culture and reputation.

Reduced healthcare costs associated with mental health conditions.

Conclusion.

Addressing mental health in the workplace is a critical aspect of creating a thriving and sustainable organization. By fostering a culture of open communication, promoting psychological safety, and providing comprehensive support, employers can empower their employees to thrive both mentally and professionally.

Ergonomics And Wellness Programs: Prioritising Employee Health

In today's competitive business landscape, organizations are increasingly recognizing the value of prioritizing employee health and well-being. A healthy and engaged workforce is not only more productive and efficient but also more resilient and adaptable to changing business demands. Embracing a holistic approach to employee health involves integrating ergonomics and wellness programs into the workplace.

Ergonomics: Designing a Safe and Comfortable Workplace.

Ergonomics is the science of designing workplaces and equipment to fit the needs of the workers. By incorporating ergonomic principles, employers can minimize the risk of musculoskeletal disorders (MSDs) and other work-related injuries. This includes factors such as:

Workstation setup: Proper height and positioning of desks, chairs, and other work surfaces to reduce strain on the neck, shoulders, back, and wrists.

Repetitive tasks: Optimizing task sequences and providing breaks to prevent fatigue and overuse injuries.

Manual lifting: Implementing proper lifting techniques and providing assistance when necessary to reduce the risk of back injuries.

Workplace environment: Maintaining a comfortable temperature, lighting, and noise levels to enhance productivity and well-being.

Wellness Programs: Promoting Overall Well-being

Wellness programs go beyond physical health and encompass a broader approach to employee well-being. These programs aim to promote physical fitness, mental health, and overall well-being through a range of initiatives, such as:

On-site fitness facilities: Providing access to exercise equipment, personal training, and group fitness classes to encourage regular physical activity.

Nutritional counseling: Offering guidance on healthy eating habits and providing healthy snacks or meals to promote a balanced diet.

Stress management workshops: Providing training on relaxation techniques, stress reduction exercises, and mindfulness practices to enhance mental health.

Health education and screenings: Offering regular health screenings, educational workshops, and counseling services to promote early detection and prevention of health problems.

Harnessing the Power of Ergonomics and Wellness

By integrating ergonomics and wellness programs into the workplace, organizations can cultivate a culture of employee well-being, leading to numerous benefits:

Reduced absenteeism and presenteeism: A healthier workforce experiences fewer injuries and illnesses, leading to lower absenteeism rates and increased productivity.

Improved employee morale and engagement: A focus on employee well-being fosters a positive work environment, boosting morale, engagement, and job satisfaction.

Reduced healthcare costs: By preventing work-related injuries and promoting overall health, organizations can minimize their healthcare expenses.

Enhanced productivity and profitability: A healthier, more engaged workforce translates into improved productivity, innovation, and ultimately, organizational success.

Integrating ergonomics and wellness programs into the workplace is a proactive investment in employee health, well-being, and organizational success. By creating a safe, comfortable, and supportive work environment, organizations can cultivate a thriving workforce that is resilient, adaptable, and ready to excel in the ever-changing business landscape.

Integrating Environmental Sustainability Into Occupational Safety

In today's interconnected world, it is becoming increasingly evident that environmental sustainability and occupational safety are not mutually exclusive, but rather complementary aspects of a holistic approach to workplace management. While traditional health and safety concerns often focus on immediate hazards and physical risks, integrating environmental sustainability into occupational safety practices broadens the scope to encompass the broader working environment and its impact on overall well-being.

Addressing Common Interdependencies.

Several key areas illustrate the synergy between environmental sustainability and occupational safety. Effective waste management practices, for instance, not only reduce the environmental footprint of a workplace but also eliminate potential safety hazards associated with hazardous materials, spills, and improper waste disposal. Similarly, energy conservation measures, such as the use of efficient lighting and equipment, not only lower energy costs but also reduce the risk of electrical fires and heat-related injuries.

Harnessing the Benefits of Sustainable Practices.

The integration of environmental sustainability into occupational safety goes beyond risk mitigation and extends to the promotion of employee health and well-being. Greener workspaces with improved ventilation, natural lighting, and access to green spaces can enhance employee morale, reduce stress, and promote physical and mental health. Additionally, sustainable procurement practices, such as using non-toxic and eco-friendly materials, can minimize exposure to harmful substances and prevent occupational illnesses.

Promoting a Culture of Sustainable Safety.

To achieve a truly integrated approach, organizations must foster a culture of sustainable safety that encompasses all aspects of workplace operations. This includes raising awareness among employees about the environmental and safety benefits of sustainable practices, encouraging participation in green initiatives, and providing ongoing training and education. By embedding sustainability into the very fabric of the workplace culture, organizations can create a healthier, safer, and more sustainable work environment for all.

Embracing a Holistic Vision.

Integrating environmental sustainability into occupational safety is not just a matter of compliance or cost-saving measures; it is a strategic decision that aligns with a broader vision of responsible business practices. By recognizing the interconnectedness of environmental, social, and economic factors, organizations can create a more sustainable and equitable workplace that benefits both employees and the planet. As the world grapples with the challenges of climate change and environmental degradation, adopting a holistic approach to occupational safety that embraces sustainability is not just an option but a necessity for future success.

Chapter 7: The Future Of Workplace Safety

Emerging Trends And Technologies

The future of workplace safety is poised for significant transformation driven by technological advancements and evolving work environments. Emerging trends and technologies hold the potential to revolutionize occupational health and safety, enhancing prevention measures, streamlining risk management, and empowering workers to take proactive steps towards safety.

1. Artificial Intelligence (AI)

AI is rapidly gaining prominence in workplace safety, particularly in analyzing vast amounts of data to identify and predict potential hazards. Intelligent systems can monitor worker behavior, equipment performance, and environmental conditions to pinpoint anomalies and potential risks. AI-powered predictive analytics can anticipate issues before they escalate into accidents, allowing for timely interventions and preventive measures.

2. Internet of Things (IoT)

The IoT is weaving a network of connected devices and sensors throughout workplaces, providing real-time insights into workplace conditions and worker interactions. IoT-enabled wearable devices can monitor employee health parameters, track movements, and detect hazardous exposures, alerting supervisors and providing immediate interventions. IoT sensors in machinery and infrastructure can detect anomalies and potential breakdowns, ensuring proactive maintenance and preventing equipment-related accidents.

3. Augmented Reality (AR) and Virtual Reality (VR)

AR and VR are transforming safety training and education, providing immersive and interactive experiences that enhance knowledge retention and engagement. AR overlays digital information onto the real world, allowing workers to visualize safety procedures, identify hazards, and practice safe behaviors in virtual environments. VR immerses workers in realistic simulations of dangerous scenarios, allowing them to develop muscle memory and make informed decisions under pressure.

4. Big Data Analytics

The collection and analysis of vast amounts of safety data, from accident reports and incident logs to workplace monitoring data, is yielding valuable insights into patterns and trends. Big data analytics can identify correlations between factors and events, enabling employers to pinpoint areas for improvement, prioritize safety initiatives, and allocate resources effectively.

5. Predictive Risk Modeling

Machine learning algorithms are being employed to develop predictive risk models that assess the likelihood of accidents or incidents based on various factors, such as worker behavior, equipment status, and environmental conditions. These models can identify high-risk areas and individuals, enabling employers to focus their safety efforts on the most critical areas and individuals.

6. Personalized Safety Solutions

Technology is enabling the development of personalized safety solutions that cater to individual worker needs and preferences. AI-powered systems can analyze individual risk profiles, work patterns, and safety habits to recommend tailored safety interventions, such as additional training, equipment adjustments, or behavioral modifications.

7. Connected Safety Ecosystems

The integration of various safety technologies and data sources within a connected ecosystem is creating a holistic view of workplace safety. This interconnected approach enables real-time communication and collaboration between safety teams, workers, and external stakeholders, fostering a collaborative culture of safety.

8. Worker Empowerment and Engagement

Emerging technologies are empowering workers to take active roles in their safety. Mobile apps and wearable devices can provide workers with real-time hazard alerts, safety checklists, and training resources, enabling them to identify and address potential risks independently. Interactive safety dashboards and visualizations can foster a sense of ownership and engagement among workers.

9. Remote Monitoring and Predictive Maintenance

The remote monitoring of equipment and machinery through IoT sensors and AI-powered systems is enabling predictive maintenance, allowing for proactive repairs and addressing potential breakdowns before they cause accidents. This remote monitoring can also extend to workers, providing real-time data on health parameters and physical exertion levels, enabling interventions to prevent fatigue-related incidents.

10. Mental Well-being and Stress Management

Technology is being utilized to address the growing concern of mental well-being in the workplace. AI-powered chatbots and virtual assistants can provide confidential mental health support and counseling, while mindfulness apps and wearable devices can track stress levels and offer guided relaxation techniques.

These emerging trends and technologies are shaping the future of workplace safety, transforming the way we prevent, manage, and respond to hazards. By embracing technological advancements and fostering a culture of safety engagement, we can create workplaces that are not only compliant but also truly safe and healthy for all workers.

Global Perspectives On Occupational Health And Safety

In a world of interconnected economies and globalized industries, the pursuit of workplace safety extends far beyond national borders. As work practices evolve, technological advancements reshape industries, and labor markets expand across continents, the need for a cohesive approach to occupational health and safety becomes increasingly evident.

International Organizations and Frameworks.

The International Labour Organization (ILO), a specialized agency of the United Nations, plays a pivotal role in promoting and protecting occupational health and safety worldwide. Through conventions, recommendations, and technical assistance, the ILO establishes international standards and guidelines for national governments, employers, and workers.

The ILO's Occupational Safety and Health Convention (OSH 155), adopted in 1981, is the cornerstone of international occupational health and safety regulation. This convention outlines the basic principles and obligations for the prevention of occupational accidents and diseases, emphasizing the responsibility of employers, the role of workers' representatives, and the need for adequate national regulations and enforcement mechanisms.

Regional Cooperation and Collaboration.

Regional organizations also contribute significantly to the advancement of occupational health and safety practices. The European Union (EU), for instance, has established comprehensive directives and regulations that harmonize workplace safety standards across its member states.

This harmonized approach promotes a common level of protection for workers while fostering innovation and best practices within the EU.

Similarly, regional organizations like the Association of Southeast Asian Nations (ASEAN) and the African Union (AU) have developed frameworks and initiatives to promote occupational health and safety across their respective regions. These efforts foster knowledge sharing, capacity building, and cross-border cooperation in addressing common safety challenges.

Challenges and Opportunities.

Despite significant progress, global challenges persist in the pursuit of workplace safety. The informal sector, where millions of workers operate outside formal employment structures, often lacks adequate safety protections. Workplace hazards in developing countries may differ from those in industrialized nations, requiring tailored approaches to risk assessment and mitigation.

The rapid rise of the digital economy and the growth of the gig economy present new challenges for occupational health and safety. Remote work arrangements, decentralized teams, and the blurring lines between work and personal life demand innovative approaches to ensuring workers' well-being and preventing occupational hazards.

The Role of Technology and Innovation.

Technology plays a crucial role in enhancing occupational health and safety practices. Advanced monitoring systems, wearable devices, and predictive analytics can identify potential hazards, assess exposure risks, and provide real-time feedback to workers and employers.

The use of artificial intelligence (AI) has the potential to revolutionize occupational safety, particularly in tasks like real-time hazard identification, automated inspections, and predictive risk assessment. AI-powered systems can analyze vast amounts of data, identify patterns and trends, and provide proactive insights to prevent incidents.

The Shared Responsibility for a Safer Workplace.

Achieving a safer future for workers requires a collective effort from governments, employers, workers, and international organizations. National governments must establish robust frameworks, provide adequate resources, and enforce safety regulations effectively. Employers must prioritize safety as an integral part of their business strategy, investing in training, hazard mitigation, and a culture of safety. Workers must play an active role in recognizing and reporting hazards, advocating for their rights, and engaging in safety initiatives.

The international community must foster collaboration, knowledge sharing, and capacity building to address shared challenges and promote best practices. The exchange of expertise, the development of harmonized standards, and the support for vulnerable workers are essential steps towards a global workplace that prioritizes the health and safety of all.

As the world evolves, the pursuit of occupational health and safety must remain a top priority. By embracing technology, fostering innovation, and fostering a shared responsibility for a safer workplace, we can create a world where work is not only a means of livelihood but also a source of well-being and dignity for all.

Advocacy For Ongoing Improvement

The future of workplace safety is not merely about compliance with regulations; it is about a relentless pursuit of excellence. This requires ongoing advocacy for continuous improvement, fostering a culture of safety that permeates every aspect of the workplace.

Empowering Employees as Safety Champions.

Employees are the eyes and ears of the workplace, often the first to identify emerging hazards or unsafe practices. Empowering them to voice their concerns and participate in safety initiatives is crucial for identifying and mitigating risks before they escalate.

Leveraging Technology for Proactive Safety.

Technology offers a wealth of opportunities to enhance workplace safety. IoT devices, data analytics, and digital platforms can provide real-time insights into workplace conditions, enabling proactive hazard detection and intervention.

Collaborating Across Industries.

Sharing knowledge and best practices across industries can accelerate the pace of safety innovation. Industry-wide collaboration fosters a sense of collective responsibility and promotes the development of standardized safety protocols and practices.

Prioritizing Prevention over Compensation.

The focus on preventing accidents and ill health should supersede the emphasis on compensation for workplace incidents. Shifting the focus to prevention incentivizes employers to invest in proactive safety measures and foster a culture of hazard elimination.

Investing in Human Capital and Training.

Providing comprehensive safety training to employees is an investment in their well-being and the overall safety of the workplace. Regular training sessions, tailored to the specific hazards of the industry, empower employees to make informed decisions and take ownership of their safety.

Enhancing Regulatory Effectiveness.

Regular reviews and updates of safety regulations are essential to address evolving workplace hazards and technological advancements. Moreover, ensuring that enforcement measures are proportionate and effective is crucial for maintaining a strong safety culture.

Engaging with Stakeholders.

Actively engaging with stakeholders, including trade unions, industry representatives, and safety experts, fosters a collaborative approach to workplace safety. Such engagement ensures that safety concerns are addressed from multiple perspectives, leading to more comprehensive and effective solutions.

Adopting a Zero-Harm Approach.

The ultimate goal of workplace safety is to achieve zero harm, a vision that inspires proactive risk management and a relentless pursuit of excellence. By embracing this approach, we can create workplaces that are truly safe and healthy for all employees.

Conclusion

Reflecting on 50 Years: Achievements, Challenges, and Unfinished Business

As we conclude this journey through 50 Years of the Health and Safety at Work Act 1974, take time to reflect on the remarkable achievements, persistent challenges, and the ongoing work that lies ahead in the realm of occupational health and safety. Over the past five decades, we have witnessed transformative changes, evolving perspectives, and the collective efforts of individuals, organizations, and communities dedicated to creating safer and healthier workplaces.

Achievements:

The accomplishments in the realm of occupational health and safety are monumental. The establishment of the Health and Safety at Work Act 1974 laid the foundation for a comprehensive legal framework that prioritizes the well-being of workers. The subsequent decades saw a paradigm shift in organizational cultures, with a growing recognition that safety is not merely a regulatory obligation but an integral aspect of ethical business practices.

Safety awareness has become ingrained in the collective consciousness, leading to the development and implementation of innovative technologies, training programs, and safety protocols. The reduction in workplace accidents, the decline in occupational diseases, and the overall improvement in safety statistics are testament to the effectiveness of concerted efforts in fostering safer working environments.

Challenges:
However, our journey also reveals persistent challenges that demand ongoing attention and collective action. Despite significant progress, workplace accidents and occupational health issues persist in certain industries and regions. The emergence of new technologies brings both opportunities and challenges, requiring continuous adaptation and vigilance to ensure that safety practices keep pace with innovation.
Mental health in the workplace remains a critical frontier, as the stigma surrounding mental health issues requires further dismantling. Global disparities in safety standards, coupled with the challenges faced by workers in developing regions, highlight the need for a more inclusive and globally responsive approach to occupational well-being.

Unfinished Business:
As we conclude this retrospective, it is evident that there is unfinished business in the pursuit of optimal workplace safety. The journey to improve and safeguard the well-being of workers is ongoing, requiring sustained commitment, innovation, and collaboration. The next 50 years hold the promise of addressing existing challenges and navigating new frontiers in occupational health and safety.

Closing Thoughts:

Reflecting on the achievements, challenges, and unfinished business prompts us to acknowledge the progress made while recognizing the collective responsibility to build upon this foundation. The commitment to workplace safety is a dynamic, evolving endeavor that requires ongoing vigilance, adaptation to emerging trends, and a dedication to fostering environments where every worker can thrive.

As we celebrate 50 years of the Health and Safety at Work Act 1974, let it serve as a reminder that our work is not complete. It is a call to action, an invitation to continue the journey "beyond compliance," shaping a future where occupational health and safety are not just regulatory requirements but ingrained principles that define the essence of work itself.

The Ongoing Journey: Commitments for the Next 50 Years

As we stand at the threshold of the next 50 years in the realm of occupational health and safety, it is essential to outline the commitments that will guide our ongoing journey. Building upon the achievements of the past and recognizing the challenges that persist, this section articulates a set of commitments to ensure that the future of workplace safety is characterized by continuous improvement, adaptability, and a steadfast dedication to the well-being of the global workforce.

Commitment 1: *Cultivating a Culture of Prevention*

Our first commitment is to cultivate a culture of prevention that permeates all levels of organizations. This involves fostering a mindset where safety is not merely a set of protocols but a collective responsibility embedded in the values and practices of every workplace. By prioritizing prevention through proactive risk assessment, continuous training, and a commitment to addressing potential hazards at their root, we pave the way for a safer and healthier future.

Commitment 2: *Embracing Technological Advancements Responsibly*

Technological advancements will continue to shape the future of work, demanding a commitment to embracing these innovations responsibly. This means integrating emerging technologies, such as artificial intelligence, wearables, and virtual reality, into safety practices while ensuring that ethical considerations, privacy concerns, and potential risks are carefully addressed. The responsible use of technology will be pivotal in enhancing safety standards and adapting to the evolving nature of work.

Commitment 3: *Prioritizing Mental Health and Well-being*

Acknowledging the significance of mental health, our commitment extends to prioritizing the well-being of the mind alongside physical safety. This involves destigmatizing mental health issues, providing comprehensive support systems, and fostering workplace cultures that prioritize open communication and mental health awareness. As we move forward, our commitment is to create environments where employees feel supported, valued, and empowered in their mental health journeys.

Commitment 4: *Global Collaboration for Universal Standards*

The pursuit of workplace safety is a global endeavor, necessitating a commitment to international collaboration. We pledge to work collaboratively with organizations, governments, and advocacy groups to establish universal standards that transcend geographical boundaries. By sharing knowledge, best practices, and resources on a global scale, we contribute to a future where every worker, regardless of location, is entitled to the highest standards of occupational health and safety.

Commitment 5: *Continuous Learning and Adaptation*

Recognizing the dynamic nature of work and safety challenges, our commitment includes a dedication to continuous learning and adaptation. This involves staying abreast of emerging trends, conducting ongoing research, and adapting safety protocols to address new and unforeseen challenges. By fostering a culture of continuous improvement, organizations can proactively respond to evolving workplace dynamics and technological advancements.

Commitment 6: *Advocacy for Worker Empowerment*

Our final commitment centers on advocacy for worker empowerment. We pledge to actively support initiatives that empower workers to voice their concerns, actively participate in safety programs, and contribute to the ongoing improvement of safety standards. Worker involvement is not just a legal requirement but a fundamental aspect of creating workplaces where every individual plays a role in shaping a safer and healthier future.

Conclusion:

The ongoing journey in occupational health and safety demands steadfast commitments to prevention, responsible technological integration, mental health prioritization, global collaboration, continuous learning, and worker empowerment. As we look ahead to the next 50 years, let these commitments guide our collective efforts in creating workplaces where every worker is valued, protected, and empowered to thrive in an environment that epitomizes the principles of safety and well-being.

APPENDIX

FULL TEXT OF THE HEALTH AND SAFETEY AT WORK ETC ACT 1974

Health and Safety at Work etc. Act 1974

1974 CHAPTER 37

An Act to make further provision for securing the health, safety and welfare of persons at work, for protecting others against risks to health or safety in connection with the activities of persons at work, for controlling the keeping and use and preventing the unlawful acquisition, possession and use of dangerous substances, and for controlling certain emissions into the atmosphere; to make further provision with respect to the employment medical advisory service; to amend the law relating to building regulations, and the Building (Scotland) Act 1959; and for connected purposes.

[31st July 1974]

BE IT ENACTED by the Queen's most Excellent Majesty, by and with the advice and consent of the Lords Spiritual and Temporal, and Commons, in this present Parliament assembled, and by the authority of the same, as follows:—

PART IHEALTH, SAFETY AND WELFARE IN CONNECTION WITH WORK, AND CONTROL OF DANGEROUS SUBSTANCES AND CERTAIN EMISSIONS INTO THE ATMOSPHERE

Preliminary

1Preliminary

(1)The provisions of this Part shall have effect with a view to—

(a)securing the health, safety and welfare of persons at work;

(b)protecting persons other than persons at work against risks to health or safety arising out of or in connection with the activities of persons at work;

(c)controlling the keeping and use of explosive or highly flammable or otherwise dangerous substances, and generally preventing the unlawful acquisition, possession and use of such substances ; and (d)controlling the emission into the atmosphere of noxious or offensive substances from premises of any class prescribed for the purposes of this paragraph.

(2)The provisions of this Part relating to the making of health and safety regulations and agricultural health and safety regulations and the preparation and approval of codes of practice shall in particular have effect with a view to enabling the enactments specified in the third column of Schedule 1 and the regulations, orders and other instruments in force under those enactments to be progressively replaced by a system of regulations and approved codes of practice operating in combination with the other provisions of this Part and designed to maintain or improve the standards of health, safety and welfare established by or under those enactments.

(3)For the purposes of this Part risks arising out of or in connection with the activities of persons at work shall be treated as including risks attributable to the manner of conducting an undertaking, the plant or substances used for the purposes of an undertaking and the condition of premises so used or any part of them.

(4)References in this Part to the general purposes of this Part are references to the purposes mentioned in subsection (1) above.

General duties

2General duties of employers to their employees

(1)It shall be the duty of every employer to ensure, so far as is reasonably practicable, the health, safety and welfare at work of all his employees.

(2)Without prejudice to the generality of an employer's duty under the preceding subsection, the matters to which that duty extends include in particular—

(a)the provision and maintenance of plant and systems of work that are, so far as is reasonably practicable, safe and without risks to health ;

(b)arrangements for ensuring, so far as is reasonably practicable, safety and absence of risks to health in connection with the use, handling, storage and transport of articles and substances ;

(c)the provision of such information, instruction, training and supervision as is necessary to ensure, so far as is reasonably practicable, the health and safety at work of his employees;

(d)so far as is reasonably practicable as regards any place of work under the employer's control, the maintenance of it in a condition that is safe and without risks to health and the provision and maintenance of means of access to and egress from it that are safe and without such risks;

(e)the provision and maintenance of a working environment for his employees that is, so far as is reasonably practicable, safe, without risks to health, and adequate as regards facilities and arrangements for their welfare at work.

(3)Except in such cases as may be prescribed, it shall be the duty of every employer to prepare and as often as may be appropriate revise a written statement of his general policy with respect to the health and safety at work of his employees and the organisation and arrangements for the time being in force for carrying out that policy, and to bring the statement and any revision of it to the notice of all of his employees.

(4)Regulations made by the Secretary of State may provide for the appointment in prescribed cases by recognised trade unions (within the meaning of the regulations) of safety representatives from amongst the employees, and those representatives shall represent the employees in consultations with the employers under subsection (6) below and shall have such other functions as may be prescribed.

(5)Regulations made by the Secretary of State may provide for the election in prescribed cases by employees of safety representatives from amongst the employees, and those representatives shall represent the employees in consultations with the employers under subsection (6) below and may have such other functions as may be prescribed.

(6)It shall be the duty of every employer to consult any such representatives with a view to the making and maintenance of arrangements which will enable him and his employees to cooperate effectively in promoting and developing measures to ensure the health and safety at work of the employees, and in checking the effectiveness of such measures.

(7)In such cases as may be prescribed it shall be the duty of every employer, if requested to do so by the safety representatives mentioned in subsections (4) and (5) above, to establish, in accordance with regulations made by the Secretary of State, a safety committee having the function of keeping under review the measures taken to ensure the health and safety at work of his employees and such other functions as may be prescribed.

3General duties of employers and self-employed to persons other than their employees

(1)It shall be the duty of every employer to conduct his undertaking in such a way as to ensure, so far as is reasonably practicable, that persons not in his employment who may be affected thereby are not thereby exposed to risks to their health or safety.

(2)It shall be the duty of every self-employed person to conduct his undertaking in such a way as to ensure, so far as is reasonably practicable, that he and other persons (not being his employees) who may be affected thereby are not thereby exposed to risks to their health or safety.

(3)In such cases as may be prescribed, it shall be the duty of every employer and every self-employed person, in the prescribed circumstances and in the prescribed manner, to give to persons (not being his employees) who may be affected by the way in which he conducts his undertaking the prescribed information about such aspects of the way in which he conducts his undertaking as might affect their health or safety.

4General duties of persons concerned with premises to persons other than their employees

(1)This section has effect for imposing on persons duties in relation to those who—

(a)are not their employees ; but

(b)use non-domestic premises made available to them as a place of work or as a place where they may use plant or substances provided for their use there,

and applies to premises so made available and other non-domestic premises used in connection with them.

(2)It shall be the duty of each person who has, to any extent, control of premises to which this section applies or of the means of access thereto or egress therefrom or of any plant or substance in such premises to take such measures as it is reasonable for a person in his position to take to ensure, so far as is reasonably practicable, that the premises, all means of access thereto or egress therefrom available for use by persons using the premises, and any plant or substance in the premises or, as the case may be, provided for use there, is or are safe and without risks to health.

(3)Where a person has, by virtue of any contract or tenancy, an obligation of any extent in relation to—

(a)the maintenance or repair of any premises to which this section applies or any means of access thereto or egress therefrom; or

(b)the safety of or the absence of risks to health arising from plant or substances in any such premises ;

that person shall be treated, for the purposes of subsection (2) above, as being a person who has control of the matters to which his obligation extends.

(4)Any reference in this section to a person having control of any premises or matter is a reference to a person having control of the premises or matter in connection with the carrying on by him of a trade, business or other undertaking (whether for profit or not).

5General duty of persons in control of certain premises in relation to harmful emissions into atmosphere

(1)It shall be the duty of the person having control of any premises of a class prescribed for the purposes of section 1(1)(d) to use the best practicable means for preventing the emission into the atmosphere from the premises of noxious or offensive substances and for rendering harmless and inoffensive such substances as may be so emitted.

(2)The reference in subsection (1) above to the means to be used for the purposes there mentioned includes a reference to the manner in which the plant provided for those purposes is used and to the supervision of any operation involving the emission of the substances to which that subsection applies.

(3)Any substance or a substance of any description prescribed for the purposes of subsection (1) above as noxious or offensive shall be a noxious or, as the case may be, an offensive substance for those purposes whether or not it would be so apart from this subsection.

(4)Any reference in this section to a person having control of any premises is a reference to a person having control of the premises in connection with the carrying on by him of a trade, business or other undertaking (whether for profit or not) and any duty imposed on any such person by this section shall extend only to matters within his control.

6General duties of manufacturers etc. as regards articles and substances for use at work

(1)It shall be the duty of any person who designs, manufactures, imports or supplies any article for use at work—

(a)to ensure, so far as is reasonably practicable, that the article is so designed and constructed as to be safe and without risks to health when properly used ;

(b)to carry out or arrange for the carrying out of such testing and examination as may be necessary for the performance of the duty imposed on him by the preceding paragraph;

(c)to take such steps as are necessary to secure that there will be available in connection with the use of the article at work adequate information about the use for which it is designed and has been tested, and about any conditions necessary to ensure that, when put to that use, it will be safe and without risks to health.

(2)It shall be the duty of any person who undertakes the design or manufacture of any article for use at work to carry out or arrange for the carrying out of any necessary research with a view to the discovery and, so far as is reasonably practicable, the elimination or minimisation of any risks to health or safety to which the design or article may give rise.

(3)It shall be the duty of any person who erects or installs any article for use at work in any premises where that article is to be used by persons at work to ensure, so far as is reasonably practicable, that nothing about the way in which it is erected or installed makes it unsafe or a risk to health when properly used.

(4)It shall be the duty of any person who manufactures, imports or supplies any substance for use at work—

(a)to ensure, so far as is reasonably practicable, that the substance is safe and without risks to health when properly used;

(b)to carry out or arrange for the carrying out of such testing and examination as may be necessary for the performance of the duty imposed on him by the preceding paragraph;

(c)to take such steps as are necessary to secure that there will be available in connection with the use of the substance at work adequate information about the results of any relevant tests which have been carried out on or in connection with the substance and about any conditions necessary to ensure that it will be safe and without risks to health when properly used.

(5)It shall be the duty of any person who undertakes the manufacture of any substance for use at work to carry out or arrange for the carrying out of any necessary research with a view to the discovery and, so far as is reasonably practicable, the elimination or minimisation of any risks to health or safety to which the substance may give rise.

(6)Nothing in the preceding provisions of this section shall be taken to require a person to repeat any testing, examination or research which has been carried out otherwise than by him or at his instance, in so far as it is reasonable for him to rely on the results thereof for the purposes of those provisions.

(7)Any duty imposed on any person by any of the preceding provisions of this section shall extend only to things done in the course of a trade, business or other undertaking carried on by him (whether for profit or not) and to matters within his control.

(8)Where a person designs, manufactures, imports or supplies an article for or to another on the basis of a written undertaking by that other to take specified steps sufficient to ensure, so far as is reasonably practicable, that the article will be safe and without risks to health when properly used, the undertaking shall have the effect of relieving the first-mentioned person from the duty imposed by subsection (1)(a) above to such extent as is reasonable having regard to the terms of the undertaking.

(9)Where a person (" the ostensible supplier ") supplies any article for use at work or substance for use at work to another (" the customer ") under a hire-purchase agreement, conditional sale agreement or credit-sale agreement, and the ostensible supplier—

(a)carries on the business of financing the acquisition of goods by others by means of such agreements; and

(b)in the course of that business acquired his interest in the article or substance supplied to the customer as a means of financing its acquisition by the customer from a third person (" the effective supplier "),

the effective supplier and not the ostensible supplier shall be treated for the purposes of this section as supplying the article or substance to the customer, and any duty imposed by the preceding provisions of this section on suppliers shall accordingly fall on the effective supplier and not on the ostensible supplier.

(10)For the purposes of this section an article or substance is not to be regarded as properly used where it is used without regard to any relevant information or advice relating to its use which has been made available by a person by whom it was designed, manufactured, imported or supplied.

7General duties of employees at work

It shall be the duty of every employee while at work—

(a)to take reasonable care for the health and safety of himself and of other persons who may be affected by his acts or omissions at work; and

(b)as regards any duty or requirement imposed on his employer or any other person by or under any of the relevant statutory provisions, to co-operate with him so far as is necessary to enable that duty or requirement to be performed or complied with.

8Duty not to interfere with or misuse things provided pursuant to certain provisions

No person shall intentionally or recklessly interfere with or misuse anything provided in the interests of health, safety or welfare in pursuance of any of the relevant statutory provisions.

9Duty not to charge employees for things done or provided pursuant to certain specific requirements

No employer shall levy or permit to be levied on any employee of his any charge in respect of anything done or provided in pursuance of any specific requirement of the relevant statutory provisions.

The Health and Safety Commission and the Health and Safety Executive

10Establishment of the Commission and the Executive

(1)There shall be two bodies corporate to be called the Health and Safety Commission and the Health and Safety Executive which shall be constituted in accordance with the following provisions of this section.

(2)The Health and Safety Commission (hereafter in this Act referred to as " the Commission ") shall consist of a chairman appointed by the Secretary of State and not less than six nor more than nine other members appointed by the Secretary of State in accordance with subsection (3) below.

(3)Before appointing the members of the Commission (other than the chairman) the Secretary of State shall—

(a)as to three of them, consult such organisations representing employers as he considers appropriate ;

(b)as to three others, consult such organisations representing employees as he considers appropriate; and

(c)as to any other members he may appoint, consult such organisations representing local authorities and such other organisations, including

138

professional bodies, the activities of whose members are concerned with matters relating to any of the general purposes of this Part, as he considers appropriate.

(4)The Secretary of State may appoint one of the members to be deputy chairman of the Commission.

(5)The Health and Safety Executive (hereafter in this Act referred to as " the Executive ") shall consist of three persons of whom one shall be appointed by the Commission with the approval of the Secretary of State to be the director of the Executive and the others shall be appointed by the Commission with the like approval after consultation with the said director.

(6)The provisions of Schedule 2 shall have effect with respect to the Commission and the Executive.

(7)The functions of the Commission and of the Executive, and of their officers and servants, shall be performed on behalf of the Crown.

11General functions of the Commission and the Executive

(1)In addition to the other functions conferred on the Commission by virtue of this Act, but subject to subsection (3) below, it shall be the general duty of the Commission to do such things and make such arrangements as it considers appropriate for the general purposes of this Part except as regards matters relating exclusively to agricultural operations.

(2)It shall be the duty of the Commission, except as aforesaid—

(a)to assist and encourage persons concerned with matters relevant to any of the general purposes of this Part to further those purposes;

(b)to make such arrangements as it considers appropriate for the carrying out of research, the publication of the results of research and the provision of training and information in connection with those purposes, and to encourage research and the provision of training and information in that connection by others ;

(c)to make such arrangements as it considers appropriate for securing that government departments, employers, employees, organisations representing employers and employees respectively, and other persons concerned with matters relevant to any of those purposes are provided with an information and advisory service and are kept informed of, and adequately advised on, such matters;

(d)to submit from time to time to the authority having power to make regulations under any of the relevant statutory provisions such proposals as the Commission considers appropriate for the making of regulations under that power.

(3)It shall be the duty of the Commission—

(a)to submit to the Secretary of State from time to time particulars of what it proposes to do for the purpose of performing its functions ; and

(b)subject to the following paragraph, to ensure that its activities are in accordance with proposals approved by the Secretary of State; and

(c)to give effect to any directions given to it by the Secretary of State.

(4)In addition to any other functions conferred on the Executive by virtue of this Part, it shall be the duty of the Executive—

(a)to exercise on behalf of the Commission such of the Commission's functions as the Commission directs it to exercise; and

(b)to give effect to any directions given to it by the Commission otherwise than in pursuance of paragraph (a) above;

but, except for the purpose of giving effect to directions given to the Commission by the Secretary of State, the Commission shall not give to the Executive any directions as to the enforcement of any of the relevant statutory provisions in a particular case.

(5)Without prejudice to subsection (2) above, it shall be the duty of the Executive, if so requested by a Minister of the Crown—

(a)to provide him with information about the activities of the Executive in connection with any matter with which he is concerned ; and

(b)to provide him with advice on any matter with which he is concerned on which relevant expert advice is obtainable from any of the officers or servants of the Executive but which is not relevant to any of the general purposes of this Part.

(6)The Commission and the Executive shall, subject to any directions given to it in pursuance of this Part, have power to do anything (except borrow money) which is calculated to facilitate, or is conducive or incidental to, the performance of any function of the Commission or, as the case may be, the Executive (including a function conferred on it by virtue of this subsection).

12Control of the Commission by the Secretary of State

The Secretary of State may—

(a)approve, with or without modifications, any proposals submitted to him in pursuance of section 11 (3)(a);

(b)give to the Commission at any time such directions as he thinks fit with respect to its functions (including directions modifying its functions, but not directions conferring on it functions other than any of which it was deprived by previous directions given by virtue of this paragraph), and any directions which it appears to him requisite or expedient to give in the interests of the safety of the State.

13Other powers of the Commission

(1)The Commission shall have power—

(a)to make agreements with any government department or other person for that department or person to perform on behalf of the Commission or the Executive (with or without payment) any of the functions of the Commission or, as the case may be, of the Executive;

(b)subject to subsection (2) below, to make agreements with any Minister of the Crown, government department or other public authority for the Commission to perform on behalf of that Minister, department or authority (with or without payment) functions exercisable by the Minister, department or authority (including, in the case of a Minister, functions not conferred by an enactment), being functions which in the opinion of the Secretary of State can appropriately be performed by the Commission in connection with any of the Commission's functions;

(c)to provide (with or without payment) services or facilities required otherwise than for the general purposes of this Part in so far as they are required by any government department or other public authority in connection with the exercise by that department or authority of any of its functions;

(d)to appoint persons or committees of persons to provide the Commission with advice in connection with any of its functions and (without prejudice to the generality of the following paragraph) to pay to persons so appointed such remuneration as the Secretary of State may with the approval of the Minister for the Civil Service determine;

(e)in connection with any of the functions of the Commission, to pay to any person such travelling and subsistence allowances and such compensation for loss of remunerative time as the Secretary of State may with the approval of the Minister for the Civil Service determine;

(f)to carry out or arrange for or make payments in respect of research into any matter connected with any of the Commission's functions, and to disseminate or arrange for or make payments in respect of the dissemination of information derived from such research ;

(g)to include, in any arrangements made by the Commission for the provision of facilities or services by it or on its behalf, provision for the making of payments to the Commission or any person acting on its behalf by other parties to the arrangements and by persons who use those facilities or services.

(2)Nothing in subsection (1)(b) shall authorise the Commission to perform any function of a Minister, department or authority which consists of a power to make regulations or other instruments of a legislative character.

14Power of the Commission to direct investigations and inquiries

(1)This section applies to the following matters, that is to say any accident, occurrence, situation or other matter whatsoever which the Commission thinks it necessary or expedient to investigate for any of the general purposes of this Part or with a view to the making of regulations for those purposes; and for the purposes of this subsection it is immaterial whether the Executive is or is not responsible for securing the enforcement of such (if any) of the relevant statutory provisions as relate to the matter in question.

(2)The Commission may at any time—

(a)direct the Executive or authorise any other person to investigate and make a special report on any matter to which this section applies ; or

(b)with the consent of the Secretary of State direct an inquiry to be held into any such matter;

but shall not do so in any particular case that appears to the Commission to involve only matters relating exclusively to agricultural operations.

(3)Any inquiry held by virtue of subsection (2)(b) above shall be held in accordance with regulations made for the purposes of this subsection by the

Secretary of State, and shall be held in public except where or to the extent that the regulations provide otherwise.

(4)Regulations made for the purposes of subsection (3) above may in particular include provision—

(a)conferring on the person holding any such inquiry, and any person assisting him in the inquiry, powers of entry and inspection;

(b)conferring on any such person powers of summoning witnesses to give evidence or produce documents and power to take evidence on oath and administer oaths or require the making of declarations ;

(c)requiring any such inquiry to be held otherwise than in public where or to the extent that a Minister of the Crown so directs.

(5)In the case of a special report made by virtue of subsection (2)(a) above or a report made by the person holding an inquiry held by virtue of subsection (2)(b) above, the Commission may cause the report, or so much of it as the Commission thinks fit, to be made public at such time and in such manner as the Commission thinks fit.

(6)The Commission—

(a)in the case of an investigation and special report made by virtue of subsection (2)(a) above (otherwise than by an officer or servant of the Executive), may pay to the person making it such remuneration and expenses as the Secretary of State may, with the approval of the Minister for the Civil Service, determine;

(b)in the case of an inquiry held by virtue of subsection (2)(b) above, may pay to the person holding it and to any assessor appointed to assist him such remuneration and expenses, and to persons attending the inquiry as witnesses such expenses, as the Secretary of State may, with the like approval, determine ; and (c)may, to such extent as the Secretary of State may determine, defray the other costs, if any, of any such investigation and special report or inquiry.

(7)Where an inquiry is directed to be held by virtue of subsection (2)(b) above into any matter to which this section applies arising in Scotland, being a matter which causes the death of any person, no inquiry with regard to that death shall, unless the Lord Advocate otherwise directs, be held in pursuance of the [1895 c. 36.] Fatal Accidents Inquiry (Scotland) Act 1895.

Health and safety regulations and approved codes of practice

15Health and safety regulations

(1)Subject to the provisions of section 50, the Secretary of State shall have power to make regulations under this section (in this part referred to as " health and safety regulations ") for any of the general purposes of this Part except as regards matters relating exclusively to agricultural operations.

(2)Without prejudice to the generality of the preceding subsection, health and safety regulations may for any of the general purposes of this Part make provision for any of the purposes mentioned in Schedule 3.

(3)Health and safety regulations—

(a)may repeal or modify any of the existing statutory provisions;

(b)may exclude or modify in relation to any specified class of case any of the provisions of sections 2 to 9 or any of the existing statutory provisions;

(c)may make a specified authority or class of authorities responsible, to such extent as may be specified, for the enforcement of any of the relevant statutory provisions.

(4)Health and safety regulations—

(a)may impose requirements by reference to the approval of the Commission or any other specified body or person;

(b)may provide for references in the regulations to any specified document to operate as references to that document as revised or re-issued from time to time.

(5)Health and safety regulations—

(a)may provide (either unconditionally or subject to conditions, and with or without limit of time) for exemptions from any requirement or prohibition imposed by or under any of the relevant statutory provisions;

(b)may enable exemptions from any requirement or prohibition imposed by or under any of the relevant statutory provisions to be granted (either unconditionally or subject to conditions, and with or without limit of time) by any specified person or by any person authorised in that behalf by a specified authority.

(6)Health and safety regulations—

(a)may specify the persons or classes of persons who, in the event of a contravention of a requirement or prohibition imposed by or under the regulations, are to be guilty of an offence, whether in addition to or to the exclusion of other persons or classes of persons;

(b)may provide for any specified defence to be available in proceedings for any offence under the relevant statutory provisions either generally or in specified circumstances;

(c)may exclude proceedings on indictment in relation to offences consisting of a contravention of a requirement or prohibition imposed by or under any of the existing statutory provisions, sections 2 to 9 or health and safety regulations;

(d)may restrict the punishments which can be imposed in respect of any such offence as is mentioned in paragraph (c) above.

(7)Without prejudice to section 35, health and safety regulations may make provision for enabling offences under any of the relevant statutory provisions to be treated as having been committed at any specified place for the purpose of bringing any such offence within the field of responsibility of any enforcing authority or conferring jurisdiction on any court to entertain proceedings for any such offence.

(8)Health and safety regulations may take the form of regulations applying to particular circumstances only or to a particular case only (for example, regulations applying to particular premises only).

(9)If an Order in Council is made under section 84(3) providing that this section shall apply to or in relation to persons, premises or work outside Great Britain then, notwithstanding the Order, health and safety regulations shall not apply to or in relation to aircraft in flight, vessels, hovercraft or offshore installations outside Great Britain or persons at work outside Great Britain in connection with submarine cables or submarine pipelines except in so far as the regulations expressly so provide.

(10)In this section " specified " means specified in health and safety regulations.

16Approval of codes of practice by the Commission

(1)For the purpose of providing practical guidance with respect to the requirements of any provision of sections 2 to 7 or of health and safety regulations or of any of the existing statutory provisions, the Commission may, subject to the following subsection and except as regards matters relating exclusively to agricultural operations—

(a)approve and issue such codes of practice (whether prepared by it or not) as in its opinion are suitable for that purpose;

(b)approve such codes of practice issued or proposed to be issued otherwise than by the Commission as in its opinion are suitable for that purpose.

(2)The Commission shall not approve a code of practice under subsection (1) above without the consent of the Secretary of State, and shall, before seeking his consent, consult—

(a)any government department or other body that appears to the Commission to be appropriate (and, in particular, in the case of a code relating to electromagnetic radiations, the National Radiological Protection Board); and

(b)such government departments and other bodies, if any, as in relation to any matter dealt with in the code, the Commission is required to consult under this section by virtue of directions given to it by the Secretary of State.

(3)Where a code of practice is approved by the Commission under subsection (1) above, the Commission shall issue a notice in writing—

(a)identifying the code in question and stating the date on which its approval by the Commission is to take effect; and

(b)specifying for which of the provisions mentioned in subsection (1) above the code is approved.

(4)The Commission may—

(a)from time to time revise the whole or any part of any code of practice prepared by it in pursuance of this section;

(b)approve any revision or proposed revision of the whole or any part of any code of practice for the time being approved under this section ;

and the provisions of subsections (2) and (3) above shall, with the necessary modifications, apply in relation to the approval of any revision under this subsection as they apply in relation to the approval of a code of practice under subsection (1) above.

(5)The Commission may at any time with the consent of the Secretary of State withdraw its approval from any code of practice approved under this section, but before seeking his consent shall consult the same government departments and other bodies as it would be required to consult under subsection (2) above if it were proposing to approve the code.

(6)Where under the preceding subsection the Commission withdraws its approval from a code of practice approved under this section, the Commission shall issue a notice in writing identifying the code in question and stating the date on which its approval of it is to cease to have effect.

(7)References in this Part to an approved code of practice are references to that code as it has effect for the time being by virtue of any revision of the whole or any part of it approved under this section.

(8)The power of the Commission under subsection (1)(b) above to approve a code of practice issued or proposed to be issued otherwise than by the Commission shall include power to approve a part of such a code of practice; and accordingly in this Part "code of practice" may be read as including a part of such a code of practice.

17Use of approved codes of practice in criminal proceedings

(1)A failure on the part of any person to observe any provision of an approved code of practice shall not of itself render him liable to any civil or criminal proceedings ; but where in any criminal proceedings a party is alleged to have committed an offence by reason of a contravention of any requirement or prohibition imposed by or under any such provision as is mentioned in section 16(1) being a provision for which there was an approved code of practice at the time of the alleged contravention, the following subsection shall have effect with respect to that code in relation to those proceedings.

(2)Any provision of the code of practice which appears to the court to be relevant to the requirement or prohibition alleged to have been contravened shall be admissible in evidence in the proceedings; and if it is proved that there was at any material time a failure to observe any provision of the code which appears to the court to be relevant to any matter which it is necessary for the prosecution to prove in order to establish a contravention of that requirement or prohibition, that matter shall be taken as proved unless the court is satisfied that the requirement or prohibition was in respect of that matter complied with otherwise than by way of observance of that provision of the code.

(3)In any criminal proceedings—

(a)a document purporting to be a notice issued by the Commission under section 16 shall be taken to be such a notice unless the contrary is proved; and

(b)a code of practice which appears to the court to be the subject of such a notice shall be taken to be the subject of that notice unless the contrary is proved.

Enforcement

18Authorities responsible for enforcement of the relevant statutory provisions

(1)It shall be the duty of the Executive to make adequate arrangements for the enforcement of the relevant statutory provisions except to the extent that some other authority or class of authorities is by any of those provisions or by regulations under subsection (2) below made responsible for their enforcement.

(2)The Secretary of State may by regulations—

(a)make local authorities responsible for the enforcement of the relevant statutory provisions to such extent as may be prescribed;

(b)make provision for enabling responsibility for enforcing any of the relevant statutory provisions to be, to such extent as may be determined under the regulations-

(i)transferred from the Executive to local authorities or from local authorities to the Executive; or (ii)assigned to the Executive or to local authorities for the purpose of removing any uncertainty as to what are by virtue of this subsection their respective responsibilities for the enforcement of those provisions:

and any regulations made in pursuance of paragraph (b) above shall include provision for securing that any transfer or assignment effected under the regulations is brought to the notice of persons affected by it.

(3)Any provision made by regulations under the preceding subsection shall have effect subject to any provision made by health and safety regulations or agricultural health and safety regulations in pursuance of section 15(3)(c).

(4)It shall be the duty of every local authority—

(a)to make adequate arrangements for the enforcement within their area of the relevant statutory provisions to the extent that they are by any of those provisions or by regulations under subsection (2) above made responsible for their enforcement; and

(b)to perform the duty imposed on them by the preceding paragraph and any other functions conferred on them by any of the relevant statutory provisions in accordance with such guidance as the Commission may give them.

(5)Where any authority other than the appropriate Agriculture Minister, the Executive or a local authority is by any of the relevant statutory provisions or by regulations under subsection (2) above made responsible for the enforcement of any of those provisions to any extent, it shall be the duty of that authority—

(a)to make adequate arrangements for the enforcement of those provisions to that extent; and

(b)to perform the duty imposed on the authority by the preceding paragraph and any other functions conferred on the authority by any of the relevant statutory provisions in accordance with such guidance as the Commission may give to the authority.

(6)Nothing in the provisions of this Act or of any regulations made thereunder charging any person in Scotland with the enforcement of any of the relevant statutory provisions shall be construed as authorising that person to institute proceedings for any offence.

(7)In this Part—

(a)"enforcing authority" means the Executive or any other authority which is by any of the relevant statutory provisions or by regulations under subsection (2) above made responsible for the enforcement of any of those provisions to any extent; and

(b)any reference to an enforcing authority's field of responsibility is a reference to the field over which that authority's responsibility for the enforcement of those provisions extends for the time being ;

but where by virtue of paragraph (a) of section 13(1) the performance of any function of the Commission or the Executive is delegated to a government department or person, references to the Commission or the Executive (or to an enforcing authority where that authority is the Executive) in any provision of this Part which relates to that function shall, so far as may be necessary to give effect to any agreement under that paragraph, be construed as references to that department or person; and accordingly any reference to the field of responsibility of an enforcing authority shall be construed as a reference to the field over which that department or person for the time being performs such a function.

19Appointment of inspectors

(1)Every enforcing authority may appoint as inspectors (under whatever title it may from time to time determine) such persons having suitable qualifications as it thinks necessary for carrying into effect the relevant statutory provisions within its field of responsibility, and may terminate any appointment made under this section.

(2)Every appointment of a person as an inspector under this section shall be made by an instrument in writing specifying which of the powers conferred on inspectors by the relevant statutory provisions are to be exercisable by the person appointed; and an inspector shall in right of his appointment under this section—

(a)be entitled to exercise only such of those powers as are so specified ; and

(b)be entitled to exercise the powers so specified only within the field of responsibility of the authority which appointed him.

(3)So much of an inspector's instrument of appointment as specifies the powers which he is entitled to exercise may be varied by the enforcing authority which appointed him.

(4)An inspector shall, if so required when exercising or seeking to exercise any power conferred on him by any of the relevant statutory provisions, produce his instrument of appointment or a duly authenticated copy thereof.

20Powers of inspectors

(1)Subject to the provisions of section 19 and this section, an inspector may, for the purpose of carrying into effect any of the relevant statutory provisions within the field of responsibility of the enforcing authority which appointed him, exercise the powers set out in subsection (2) below.

(2)The powers of an inspector referred to in the preceding subsection are the following, namely—

(a)at any reasonable time (or, in a situation which in his opinion is or may be dangerous, at any time) to enter any premises which he has reason co believe it is necessary for him to enter for the purpose mentioned in subsection (1) above ;

(b)to take with him a constable if he has reasonable cause to apprehend any serious obstruction in the execution of his duty;

(c)without prejudice to the preceding paragraph, on entering any premises by virtue of paragraph (a) above to take with him—

(i)any other person duly authorised by his (the inspector's) enforcing authority ; and

(ii)any equipment or materials required for any purpose for which the power of entry is being exercised;

(d)to make such examination and investigation as may in any circumstances be necessary for the purpose mentioned in subsection (1) above ;

(e)as regards any premises which he has power to enter, to direct that those premises or any part of them, or anything therein, shall be left undisturbed (whether generally or in particular respects) for so long as is reasonably necessary for the purpose of any examination or investigation under paragraph (d) above;

(f)to take such measurements and photographs and make such recordings as he considers necessary for the purpose of any examination or investigation under paragraph (d) above;

(g)to take samples of any articles or substances found in any premises which he has power to enter, and of the atmosphere in or in the vicinity of any such premises ;

(h)in the case of any article or substance found in any premises which he has power to enter, being an article or substance which appears to him to have caused or to be likely to cause danger to health or safety, to cause it to be dismantled or subjected to any process or test (but not so as to damage or destroy it unless this is in the circumstances necessary for the purpose mentioned in subsection (1) above);

(i)in the case of any such article or substance as is mentioned in the preceding paragraph, to take possession of it and detain it for so long as is necessary for all or any of the following purposes, namely—

(i)to examine it and do to it anything which he has power to do under that paragraph ;

(ii)to ensure that it is not tampered with before his examination of it is completed ;

(iii)to ensure that it is available for use as evidence in any proceedings for an offence under any of the relevant statutory provisions or any proceedings relating to a notice under section 21 or 22;

(j)to require any person whom he has reasonable cause to believe to be able to give any information relevant to any examination or investigation under paragraph (d) above to answer (in the absence of persons other than a person nominated by him to be present and any persons whom the inspector may allow to be present) such questions as the inspector thinks fit to ask and to sign a declaration of the truth of his answers ;

(k)to require the production of, inspect, and take copies of or of any entry in—

(i)any books or documents which by virtue of any of the relevant statutory provisions are required to be kept; and

(ii)any other books or documents which it is necessary for him to see for the purposes of any examination or investigation under paragraph (d) above;

(l)to require any person to afford him such facilities and assistance with respect to any matters or things within that person's control or in relation to which that person has responsibilities as are necessary to enable the inspector to exercise any of the powers conferred on him by this section ;

(m)any other power which is necessary for the purpose mentioned in subsection (1) above.

(3)The Secretary of State may by regulations make provision as to the procedure to be followed in connection with the taking of samples under subsection (2)(g) above (including provision as to the way in which samples that have been so taken are to be dealt with).

(4)Where an inspector proposes to exercise the power conferred by subsection (2)(h) above in the case of an article or substance found in any premises, he shall, if so requested by a person who at the time is present in and has responsibilities in relation to those premises, cause anything which is to be done by virtue of that power to be done in the presence of that person unless the inspector considers that its being done in that person's presence would be prejudicial to the safety of the State.

(5)Before exercising the power conferred by subsection (2)(h) above in the case of any article or substance, an inspector shall consult such persons as appear to him appropriate for the purpose of ascertaining what dangers, if any, there may be in doing anything which he proposes to do under that power.

(6)Where under the power conferred by subsection (2)(i) above an inspector takes possession of any article or substance found in any premises, he shall leave there, either with a responsible person or, if that is impracticable, fixed in a conspicuous position, a notice giving particulars of that article or substance sufficient to identify it and stating that he has taken possession of it under that power; and before taking possession of any such substance under that power an inspector shall, if it is practicable for him to do so, take a sample thereof and give to a responsible person at the premises a portion of the sample marked in a manner sufficient to identify it.

(7)No answer given by a person in pursuance of a requirement imposed under subsection (2)(j) above shall be admissible in evidence against that person or the husband or wife of that person in any proceedings.

(8)Nothing in this section shall be taken to compel the production by any person of a document of which he would on grounds of legal professional privilege be entitled to withhold production on an order for discovery in an action in the High Court or, as the case may be, on an order for the production of documents in an action in the Court of Session.

21Improvement notices

If an inspector is of the opinion that a person—

(a)is contravening one or more of the relevant statutory provisions; or

(b)has contravened one or more of those provisions in circumstances that make it likely that the contravention will continue or be repeated,

he may serve on him a notice (in this Part referred to as " an improvement notice ") stating that he is of that opinion, specifying the provision or provisions as to which he is of that opinion, giving particulars of the reasons why he is of that opinion, and requiring that person to remedy the contravention or, as the case may be, the matters occasioning it within such period (ending not earlier than the period within which an appeal against the notice can be brought under section 24) as may be specified in the notice.

22Prohibition notices

(1)This section applies to any activities which are being or are about to be carried on by or under the control of any person, being activities to or in relation to which any of the relevant statutory provisions apply or will, if the activities are so carried on, apply.

(2)If as regards any activities to which this section applies an inspector is of the opinion that, as carried on or about to be carried on by or under the control of the person in question, the activities involve or, as the case may be, will involve a risk of serious personal injury, the inspector may serve on that person a notice (in this Part referred to as " a prohibition notice ").

(3)A prohibition notice shall—

(a)state that the inspector is of the said opinion ;

(b)specify the matters which in his opinion give or, as the case may be, will give rise to the said risk ;

(c)where in his opinion any of those matters involves or, as the case may be, will involve a contravention of any of the relevant statutory provisions, state that he is of that opinion, specify the provision or provisions as to which he is of that opinion, and give particulars of the reasons why he is of that opinion ; and

(d)direct that the activities to which the notice relates shall not be carried on by or under the control of the person on whom the notice is served unless the matters specified in the notice in pursuance of paragraph (b) above and any associated contraventions of provisions so specified in pursuance of paragraph (c) above have been remedied.

(4)A direction given in pursuance of subsection (3)(d) above shall take immediate effect if the inspector is of the opinion, and states it, that the risk of serious personal injury is or, as the case may be, will be imminent, and shall have effect at the end of a period specified in the notice in any other case.

23Provisions supplementary to ss. 21 and 22

(1)In this section " a notice " means an improvement notice or a prohibition notice.

(2)A notice may (but need not) include directions as to the measures to be taken to remedy any contravention or matter to which the notice relates ; and any such directions—

(a)may be framed to any extent by reference to any approved code of practice ; and (b)may be framed so as to afford the person on whom the notice is served a choice between different ways of remedying the contravention or matter.

(3)Where any of the relevant statutory provisions applies to a building or any matter connected with a building and an inspector proposes to serve an improvement notice relating to a contravention of that provision in connection with that building or matter, the notice shall not direct any measures to be taken to remedy the contravention of that provision which are more onerous than those necessary to secure conformity with the requirements of any building regulations for the time being in force to which that building or matter would be required to conform if the relevant building were being newly erected unless the provision in question imposes specific requirements more onerous than the requirements of any such building regulations to which the building or matter would be required to conform as aforesaid.

In this subsection " the relevant building ", in the case of a building, means that building, and, in the case of a matter connected with a building, means the building with which the matter is connected.

(4)Before an inspector serves in connection with any premises used or about to be used as a place of work a notice requiring or likely to lead to the taking of measures affecting the means of escape in case of fire with which the premises are or ought to be provided, he shall consult the fire authority.

In this subsection " fire authority " has the meaning assigned by section 43(1) of the [1971 c. 40.] Fire Precautions Act 1971.

(5)Where an improvement notice or a prohibition notice which is not to take immediate effect has been served—

(a)the notice may be withdrawn by an inspector at any time before the end of the period specified therein in pursuance of section 21 or section 22(4) as the case may be; and (b)the period so specified may be extended or further extended by an inspector at any time when an appeal against the notice is not pending.

(6)In the application of this section to Scotland—

(a)in subsection (3) for the words from " with the requirements " to " aforesaid " there shall be substituted the words—

"(a)to any provisions of the building standards regulations to which that building or matter would be required to conform if the relevant building were being newly erected ; or

(b)where the sheriff, on an appeal to him under section 16 of the [1959 c. 24.] Building (Scotland) Act 1959—

(i)against an order under section 10 of that Act requiring the execution of operations necessary to make the building or matter conform to the building standards regulations, or

(ii)against an order under section 11 of that Act requiring the building or matter to conform to a provision of such regulations, has varied the order, to any provisions of the building standards regulations referred to in paragraph (a) above as affected by the order as so varied, unless the relevant statutory provision imposes specific requirements more onerous than the requirements of any provisions of building standards regulations as aforesaid or, as the case may be, than the requirements of the order as varied by the sheriff.";

(b)after subsection (5) there shall be inserted the following subsection—

"(5A)In subsection (3) above ' building standards regulations' has the same meaning as in section 3 of the Building (Scotland) Act 1959.".

24Appeal against improvement or prohibition notice

(1)In this section " a notice " means an improvement notice or a prohibition notice.

(2)A person on whom a notice is served may within such period from the date of its service as may be prescribed appeal to an industrial tribunal; and on such an appeal the tribunal may either cancel or affirm the notice and, if it affirms it, may do so either in its original form or with such modifications as the tribunal may in the circumstances think fit,

(3)Where an appeal under this section is brought against a notice within the period allowed under the preceding subsection, then—

(a)in the case of an improvement notice, the bringing of the appeal shall have the effect of suspending the operation of the notice until the appeal is finally disposed of or, if the appeal is withdrawn, until the withdrawal of the appeal;

(b)in the case of a prohibition notice, the bringing of the appeal shall have the like effect if, but only if, on the application of the appellant the tribunal so directs (and then only from the giving of the direction).

(4)One or more assessors may be appointed for the purposes of any proceedings brought before an industrial tribunal under this section.

25Power to deal with cause of imminent danger

(1)Where, in the case of any article or substance found by him in any premises which he has power to enter, an inspector has reasonable cause to believe that, in the circumstances in which he finds it, the article or substance is a cause of imminent danger of serious personal injury, he may seize it and cause it to be rendered harmless (whether by destruction or otherwise).

(2)Before there is rendered harmless under this section—

(a)any article that forms part of a batch of similar articles ; or

(b)any substance,

the inspector shall, if it is practicable for him to do so, take a sample thereof and give to a responsible person at the premises where the article or substance was found by him a portion of the sample marked in a manner sufficient to identify it.

(3)As soon as may be after any article or substance has been seized and rendered harmless under this section, the inspector shall prepare and sign a written report giving particulars of the circumstances in which the article or substance was seized and so dealt with by him, and shall—

(a)give a signed copy of the report to a responsible person at the premises where the article or substance was found by him; and

(b)unless that person is the owner of the article or substance, also serve a signed copy of the report on the owner;

and if, where paragraph (b) above applies, the inspector cannot after reasonable enquiry ascertain the name or address of the owner, the copy may be served on him by giving it to the person to whom a copy was given under the preceding paragraph.

26Power of enforcing authorities to indemnify their inspectors

Where an action has been brought against an inspector in respect of an act done in the execution or purported execution of any of the relevant statutory provisions and the circumstances are such that he is not legally entitled to require the enforcing authority which appointed him to indemnify him, that authority may, nevertheless, indemnify him against the whole or part of any damages and costs or expenses which he may have been ordered to pay or may have incurred, if the authority is satisfied that he honestly believed that the act complained of was within his powers and that his duty as an inspector required or entitled him to do it.

Obtaining and disclosure of information

27Obtaining of information by the Commission, the Executive, enforcing authorities etc.

(1)For the purpose of obtaining—

(a)any information which the Commission needs for the discharge of its functions; or

(b)any information which an enforcing authority needs for the discharge of the authority's functions,

the Commission may, with the consent of the Secretary of State, serve on any person a notice requiring that person to furnish to the Commission or, as the case may be, to the enforcing authority in question such information about such matters as may be specified in the notice, and to do so in such form and manner and within such time as may be so specified.

In this subsection " consent" includes a general consent extending to cases of any stated description.

(2)Nothing in section 9 of the [1947 c. 39.] Statistics of Trade Act 1947 (which restricts the disclosure of information obtained under that Act) shall prevent or penalise—

(a)the disclosure by a Minister of the Crown to the Commission or the Executive of information obtained under that Act about any undertaking within the meaning of that Act, being information consisting of the names and addresses of the persons carrying on the undertaking, the nature of the undertaking's activities, the numbers of persons of different descriptions who work in the undertaking, the addresses or places where activities of the undertaking are or were carried on, the nature of the activities carried on there, or the numbers of persons of different descriptions who work or worked in the undertaking there ; or (b)the disclosure by the Manpower Services Commission, the Employment Service Agency or the Training Services Agency to the Commission or the Executive of information so obtained which is of a kind specified in a notice in writing given to the disclosing body and the recipient of the information by the Secretary of State under this paragraph.

(3)In the preceding subsection any reference to a Minister of the Crown, the Commission, the Executive, the Manpower Services Commission or either of the said Agencies includes respectively a reference to an officer of his or of that body and also, in the case of a reference to the Commission, includes a reference to—

(a)a person performing any functions of the Commission or the Executive on its behalf by virtue of section 13(1)(a);

(b)an officer of a body which is so performing any such functions ; and

(c)an adviser appointed in pursuance of section 13(1)(d).

(4)A person to whom information is disclosed in pursuance of subsection (2) above shall not use the information for a purpose other than a purpose of the Commission or, as the case may be, of the Executive.

28Restrictions on disclosure of information

(1)In this and the two following subsections—

(a)" relevant information" means information obtained by a person under section 27(1) or furnished to any person in pursuance of a requirement imposed by any of the relevant statutory provisions; and

(b)" the recipient ", in relation to any relevant information, means the person by whom that information was so obtained or to whom that information was so furnished, as the case may be.

(2)Subject to the following subsection, no relevant information shall be disclosed without the consent of the person by whom it was furnished.

(3)The preceding subsection shall not apply to—

(a)disclosure of information to the Commission, the Executive, a government department or any enforcing authority;

(b)without prejudice to paragraph (a) above, disclosure by the recipient of information to any person for the purpose of any function conferred on the recipient by or under any of the relevant statutory provisions;

(c)without prejudice to paragraph (a) above, disclosure by the recipient of information to—

(i)an officer of a local authority who is authorised by that authority to receive it,

(ii)an officer of a water authority or water development board who is authorised by that authority or board to receive it,

(iii)an officer of a river purification board who is authorised by that board to receive it, or

(iv)a constable authorised by a chief officer of police to receive it;

(d)disclosure by the recipient of information in a form calculated to prevent it from being identified as relating to a particular person or case ;

(e)disclosure of information for the purposes of any legal proceedings or any investigation or inquiry held by virtue of section 14(2), or for the purposes of a report of any such proceedings or inquiry or of a special report made by virtue of section 14(2).

(4)In the preceding subsection any reference to the Commission, the Executive, a government department or an enforcing authority includes respectively a reference to an officer of that body or authority (including, in the case of an enforcing authority, any inspector appointed by it), and also, in the case of a reference to the Commission, includes a reference to—

(a)a person performing any functions of the Commission or the Executive on its behalf by virtue of section 13(1)(a);

(b)an officer of a body which is so performing any such functions; and

(c)an adviser appointed in pursuance of section 13(1)(d).

(5)A person to whom information is disclosed in pursuance of subsection (3) above shall not use the information for a purpose other than—

(a)in a case falling within paragraph (a) of that subsection, a purpose of the Commission or of the Executive or of the government department in question, or the purposes of the enforcing authority in question in connection with the relevant statutory provisions, as the case may be;

(b)in the case of information given to an officer of a local authority or of a water authority or of a river purification board or water development board, the purposes of the authority or board in connection with the relevant statutory provisions or any enactment whatsoever relating to public health, public safety or the protection of the environment;

(c)in the case of information given to a constable, the purposes of the police in connection with the relevant statutory provisions or any enactment whatsoever relating to public health, public safety or the safety of the State.

(6)In subsections (3)(c) and (5) above, before 16th May 1975, the references to a water authority in their application to Scotland shall be construed as references to a regional water board.

(7)A person shall not disclose any information obtained by him as a result of the exercise of any power conferred by section 14(4)(a) or 20 (including, in particular, any information with respect to any trade secret obtained by him in any premises entered by him by virtue of any such power) except—

(a)for the purposes of his functions; or

(b)for the purposes of any legal proceedings or any investigation or inquiry held by virtue of section 14(2) or for the purposes of a report of any such proceedings or inquiry or of a special report made by virtue of section 14(2); or

(c)with the relevant consent.

In this subsection " the relevant consent" means, in the case of information furnished in pursuance of a requirement imposed under section 20, the consent of the person who furnished it, and, in any other case, the consent of a person having responsibilities in relation to the premises where the information was obtained.

(8)Notwithstanding anything in the preceding subsection an inspector shall, in circumstances in which it is necessary to do so for the purpose of assisting in keeping persons (or the representatives of persons) employed at any premises adequately informed about matters affecting their health, safety and welfare, give to such persons or their representatives the following descriptions of information, that is to say—

(a)factual information obtained by him as mentioned in that subsection which relates to those premises or anything which was or is therein or was or is being done therein; and

(b)information with respect to any action which he has taken or proposes to take in or in connection with those premises in the performance of his functions;

and, where an inspector does as aforesaid, he shall give the like information to the employer of the first-mentioned persons.

Special provisions relating to agriculture

29General functions of Ministers responsible for agriculture in relation to the relevant agricultural purposes

(1)It shall be the duty of the appropriate Agriculture Minister—

(a)to do such things and make such arrangements as he considers appropriate for the relevant agricultural purposes; and

(b)to make such arrangements as he considers appropriate for securing that employers, employees, organisations representing employers and employees respectively, and other persons concerned with matters relevant to any of those purposes are kept informed of, and adequately advised on, such matters.

(2)The Minister of Agriculture, Fisheries and Food shall make an annual report to Parliament of his proceedings under the relevant statutory provisions, and may include that report in the annual report made to Parliament in pursuance of section 13 of the [1948 c. 47.] Agricultural Wages Act 1948.

(3)The Secretary of State concerned with agriculture in Scotland shall make an annual report to Parliament of his proceedings under the relevant statutory provisions.

30Agricultural health and safety regulations

(1)Regulations under this section (in this Part referred to as " agricultural health and safety regulations".) may be made for any of the relevant agricultural purposes.

(2)Agricultural health and safety regulations may be either regulations applying to Great Britain and made by the Minister of Agriculture, Fisheries and Food and the Secretary of State acting jointly, or regulations applying to England and Wales only and made by the said Minister, or regulations applying to Scotland only and made by the Secretary of State.

(3)Where health and safety regulations make provision for any purpose with respect to a matter that relates to (but not exclusively to) agricultural operations—

(a)provision for that purpose shall not be made with respect to that matter by agricultural health and safety regulations so as to have effect while the first-mentioned provision is in force except for the purpose of imposing requirements additional to those imposed by health and safety regulations, being additional requirements which in the opinion of the authority making the agricultural health and safety regulations are necessary or expedient in the special circumstances of agricultural operations; and

(b)in the event of any inconsistency between the first-mentioned provision and any provision made with respect to that matter by agricultural health and safety regulations, the first-mentioned provision shall prevail.

(4)The provisions of section 15(2) to (10) and Schedule 3 shall have effect in relation to agricultural health and safety regulations as they have effect in relation to health and safety regulations subject to the following modifications, that is to say—

(a)references to the relevant statutory provisions or the existing statutory provisions shall be read as references to such of those provisions as relate to agriculture;

(b)in section 15(4) the references to the Commission shall be read as references to the appropriate Agriculture Minister;

(c)in section 15(6) and (10) and paragraph 23 of Schedule 3, the reference to health and safety regulations shall be read as a reference to agricultural health and safety regulations.

(5)Without prejudice to the generality of subsection (1) above, agricultural health and safety regulations may, as regards agricultural licences under any of the relevant statutory provisions, make provision for requiring the authority having power to issue, renew, vary, transfer or revoke such licences to notify—

(a)any applicant for the issue, renewal, variation or transfer of such a licence of any proposed decision of the authority to refuse the application ; or

(b)the holder of such a licence of any proposed decision of the authority to revoke the licence or to vary any term, condition or restriction on or subject to which the licence is held ;

and for enabling persons aggrieved by any such proposed decision to make representations to, or to a person appointed by, the relevant authority within the period and in the manner prescribed by the regulations.

(6)In relation to any agricultural health and safety regulations made in pursuance of paragraph 2 of Schedule 3 as applied by this section, subsection (2) above shall have effect as if after the words " Great Britain " there were inserted the words " or the United Kingdom ".

31Enforcement of the relevant statutory provisions in connection with agriculture

Subject to any provision made by regulations under section 15, 18 or 30, it shall be the duty of the appropriate Agriculture Minister to make adequate arrangements for the enforcement of the relevant statutory provisions in their application to matters relating exclusively to the relevant agricultural purposes.

32Application of provisions of this Part in connection with agriculture

(1)The following provisions of this section shall have effect with a view to the application of certain provisions of this Part in relation to the Agriculture Ministers or matters relating exclusively to the relevant agricultural purposes.

(2)Subject to the following subsection—

(a)sections 13, 14, 17(3), 27 and 28 shall apply in relation to the appropriate Agriculture Minister as they apply in relation to the Commission ;

(b)section 16 shall apply in relation to matters relating exclusively to the relevant agricultural purposes as it applies in relation to other matters.

(3)In their application as provided by the preceding subsection, the provisions of this Part which are specified in the first column of Schedule 4 shall have effect subject to the modifications provided for in the second column of that Schedule.

Provisions as to offences

33Offences

(1)It is an offence for a person—

(a)to fail to discharge a duty to which he is subject by virtue of sections 2 to 7 ;

(b)to contravene section 8 or 9 ;

(c)to contravene any health and safety regulations or agricultural health and safety regulations or any requirement or prohibition imposed under any such regulations (including any requirement or prohibition to which he is subject by virtue of the terms of or any condition or restriction attached to any licence, approval, exemption or other authority issued, given or granted under the regulations);

(d)to contravene any requirement imposed by or under regulations under section 14 or intentionally to obstruct any person in the exercise of his powers under that section;

(e)to contravene any requirement imposed by an inspector under section 20 or 25 ;

(f)to prevent or attempt to prevent any other person from appearing before an inspector or from answering any question to which an inspector may by virtue of section 20(2) require an answer ;

(g)to contravene any requirement or prohibition imposed by an improvement notice or a prohibition notice (including any such notice as modified on appeal);

(h)intentionally to obstruct an inspector in the exercise or performance of his powers or duties ;

(i)to contravene any requirement imposed by a notice under section 27(1);

(j)to use or disclose any information in contravention of section 27(4) or 28 ;

(k)to make a statement which he knows to be false or recklessly to make a statement which is false where the statement is made—

(i)in purported compliance with a requirement to furnish any information imposed by or under any of the relevant statutory provisions; or

(ii)for the purpose of obtaining the issue of a document under any of the relevant statutory provisions to himself or another person ;

(l)intentionally to make a false entry in any register, book, notice or other document required by or under any of the relevant statutory provisions to be kept, served or given or, with intent to deceive, to make use of any such entry which he knows to be false ;

(m)with intent to deceive, to forge or use a document issued or authorised to be issued under any of the relevant statutory provisions or required for any purpose thereunder or to make or have in his possession a document so closely resembling any such document as to be calculated to deceive;

(n)falsely to pretend to be an inspector ;

(o)to fail to comply with an order made by a court under section 42.

(2)A person guilty of an offence under paragraph (d). (f), (h) or (n) of subsection (1) above, or of an offence under paragraph (e) of that subsection consisting of contravening a requirement imposed by an inspector under section 20, shall be liable on summary conviction to a fine not exceeding £400.

(3)Subject to any provision made by virtue of section 15(6)(d) or by virtue of paragraph 2(2) of Schedule 3, a person guilty of an offence under any paragraph of subsection (1) above not mentioned in the preceding subsection, or of an offence under subsection (1)(e) above not falling within the preceding subsection, or of an offence under any of the existing statutory provisions, being an offence for which no other penalty is specified, shall be liable—

(a)on summary conviction, to a fine not exceeding £400;

(b)on conviction on indictment—

(i)if the offence is one to which this sub-paragraph applies, to imprisonment for a term not exceeding two years, or a fine, or both ;

(ii)if the offence is not one to which the preceding sub-paragraph applies, to a fine.

(4)Subsection (3)(b)(i) above applies to the following offences—

(a)an offence consisting of contravening any of the relevant statutory provisions by doing otherwise than under the authority of a licence issued by the Executive or the appropriate Agriculture Minister something for the doing of which such a licence is necessary under the relevant statutory provisions;

(b)an offence consisting of contravening a term of or a condition or restriction attached to any such licence as is mentioned in the preceding paragraph;

(c)an offence consisting of acquiring or attempting to acquire, possessing or using an explosive article or substance (within the meaning of any of the relevant statutory provisions) in contravention of any of the relevant statutory provisions;

(d)an offence under subsection (Dig) above consisting of contravening a requirement or prohibition imposed by a prohibition notice ;

(e)an offence under subsection (1)(j) above.

(5)Where a person is convicted of an offence under subsection (1)(g) or (o) above, then, if the contravention in respect of which he was convicted is continued after the conviction he shall (subject to section 42(3)) be guilty of a further offence and liable in respect thereof to a fine not exceeding £50 for each day on which the contravention is so continued.

(6)In this section " forge " has, for England and Wales, the same meaning as in the [1913 c. 27.] Forgery Act 1913.

34Extension of time for bringing summary proceedings

(1)Where—

(a)a special report on any matter to which section 14 of this Act applies is made by virtue of subsection (2) to) of that section ; or

(b)a report is made by the person holding an inquiry into any such matter by virtue of subsection (2) (b) of that section; or

(c)a coroner's inquest is held touching the death of any person whose death may have been caused by an accident which happened while he was at work or by a disease which he contracted or probably contracted at work or by any accident, act or omission which occurred in connection with the work of any person whatsoever; or

(d)a public inquiry into any death that may have been so caused is held under the [1895 c. 36.] Fatal Accidents Inquiry (Scotland) Act 1895 or the [1906 c. 35.] Fatal Accidents and Sudden Deaths Inquiry (Scotland) Act 1906,

and it appears from the report or, in a case falling within paragraph (c) or (d) above, from the proceedings at the inquest or inquiry, that any of the relevant statutory provisions was contravened at a time which is material in relation to the subject-matter of the report, inquest or inquiry, summary proceedings against any person liable to be proceeded against in respect of the contravention may be commenced at any time within three months of the making of the report or, in a

174

case falling within paragraph (c) or (d) above, within three months of the conclusion of the inquest or inquiry.

(2)Where an offence under any of the relevant statutory provisions is committed by reason of a failure to do something at or within a time fixed by or under any of those provisions, the offence shall be deemed to continue until that thing is done.

(3)Summary proceedings for an offence to which this subsection applies may be commenced at any time within six months from the date on which there comes to the knowledge of a responsible enforcing authority evidence sufficient in the opinion of that authority to justify a prosecution for that offence ; and for the purposes of this subsection—

(a)a certificate of an enforcing authority stating that such evidence came to its knowledge on a specified date shall be conclusive evidence of that fact; and

(b)a document purporting to be such a certificate and to be signed by or on behalf of the enforcing authority in question shall be presumed to be such a certificate unless the contrary is proved.

(4)The preceding subsection applies to any offence under any of the relevant statutory provisions which a person commits by virtue of any provision or requirement to which he is subject as the designer, manufacturer, importer or supplier of any thing ; and in that subsection " responsible enforcing authority " means an enforcing authority within whose field of responsibility the offence in question lies, whether by virtue of section 35 or otherwise.

(5)In the application of subsection (3) above to Scotland—

(a)for the words from " there comes " to " that offence " there shall be substituted the words " evidence, sufficient in the opinion of the enforcing authority to justify a report to the Lord Advocate with a view to consideration of the question of prosecution, comes to the knowledge of the authority ";

(b)at the end of paragraph (b) there shall be added the words "and

(c)section 23(2) of the [1954 c. 48.] Summary Jurisdiction (Scotland) Act 1954 (date of commencement of proceedings) shall have effect as it has effect for the purposes of that section.".

35Venue

An offence under any of the relevant statutory provisions committed in connection with any plant or substance may, if necessary for the purpose of bringing the offence within the field of responsibility of any enforcing authority or conferring jurisdiction on any court to entertain proceedings for the offence, be treated as having been committed at the place where that plant or substance is for the time being.

36Offences due to fault of other person

(1)Where the commission by any person of an offence under any of the relevant statutory provisions is due to the act or default of some other person, that other person shall be guilty of the offence, and a person may be charged with and convicted of the offence by virtue of this subsection whether or not proceedings are taken against the first-mentioned person.

(2)Where there would be or have been the commission of an offence under section 33 by the Crown but for the circumstance that that section does not bind the Crown, and that fact is due to the act or default of a person other than the Crown, that person shall be guilty of the offence which, but for that circumstance, the Crown would be committing or would have committed, and may be charged with and convicted of that offence accordingly.

(3)The preceding provisions of this section are subject to any provision made by virtue of section 15(6).

37Offences by bodies corporate

(1)Where an offence under any of the relevant statutory provisions committed by a body corporate is proved to have been committed with the consent or connivance of, or to have been attributable to any neglect on the part of, any director, manager, secretary or other similar officer of the body corporate or a person who was purporting to act in any such capacity, he as well as the body corporate shall be guilty of that offence and shall be liable to be proceeded against and punished accordingly.

(2)Where the affairs of a body corporate are managed by its members, the preceding subsection shall apply in relation to the acts and defaults of a member in connection with his functions of management as if he were a director of the body corporate.

38Restriction on institution of proceedings in England and Wales

Proceedings for an offence under any of the relevant statutory provisions shall not, in England and Wales, be instituted except by an inspector or by or with the consent of the Director of Public Prosecutions.

39Prosecutions by inspectors

(1)An inspector, if authorised in that behalf by the enforcing authority which appointed him, may, although not of counsel or a solicitor, prosecute before a magistrates' court proceedings for an offence under any of the relevant statutory provisions.

(2)This section shall not apply to Scotland.

40Onus of proving limits of what is practicable etc.

In any proceedings for an offence under any of the relevant statutory provisions consisting of a failure to comply with a duty or requirement to do something so far as is practicable or so far as is reasonably practicable, or to use the best practicable means to do something, it shall be for the accused to prove (as the case may be) that it was not practicable or not reasonably practicable to do more than was in fact done to satisfy the duty or requirement, or that there was no better practicable means than was in fact used to satisfy the duty or requirement.

41Evidence

(1)Where an entry is required by any of the relevant statutory provisions to be made in any register or other record, the entry, if made, shall, as against the person by or on whose behalf it was made, be admissible as evidence or in Scotland sufficient evidence of the facts stated therein.

(2)Where an entry which is so required to be so made with respect to the observance of any of the relevant statutory provisions has not been made, that fact shall be admissible as evidence or in Scotland sufficient evidence that that provision has not been observed.

42Power of court to order cause of offence to be remedied or, in certain cases, forfeiture

(1)Where a person is convicted of an offence under any of the relevant statutory provisions in respect of any matters which appear to the court to be matters which it is in his power to remedy, the court may, in addition to or instead of imposing any punishment, order him, within such time as may be fixed by the order, to take such steps as may be specified in the order for remedying the said matters.

(2)The time fixed by an order under subsection (1) above may be extended or further extended by order of the court on an application made before the end of that time as originally fixed or as extended under this subsection, as the case may be.

(3)Where a person is ordered under subsection (1) above to remedy any matters, that person shall not be liable under any of the relevant statutory provisions in respect of those matters in so far as they continue during the time fixed by the order or any further time allowed under subsection (2) above.

(4)Subject to the following subsection, the court by or before which a person is convicted of an offence such as is mentioned in section 33(4)(c) in respect of any such explosive article or substance as is there mentioned may order the article or substance in question to be forfeited and either destroyed or dealt with in such other manner as the court may order.

(5)The court shall not order anything to be forfeited under the preceding subsection where a person claiming to be the owner of or otherwise interested in it applies to be heard by the court, unless an opportunity has been given to him to show cause why the order should not be made.

Financial provisions

43Financial provisions

(1)It shall be the duty of the Secretary of State to pay to the Commission such sums as are approved by the Treasury and as he considers appropriate for the purpose of enabling the Commission to perform its functions; and it shall be the duty of the Commission to pay to the Executive such sums as the Commission considers appropriate for the purpose of enabling the Executive to perform its functions.

(2)Regulations may provide for such fees as may be fixed by or determined under the regulations to be payable for or in connection with the performance by or on behalf of any authority to which this subsection applies of any function conferred on that authority by or under any of the relevant statutory provisions.

(3)Subsection (2) above applies to the following authorities, namely the Commission, the Executive, the Secretary of State, the Minister of Agriculture, Fisheries and Food, every enforcing authority, and any other person on whom any function is conferred by or under any of the relevant statutory provisions.

(4)Regulations under this section may specify the person by whom any fee payable under the regulations is to be paid; but no such fee shall be made payable by a person in any of the following capacities, namely an employee, a person seeking employment, a person training for employment, and a person seeking training for employment.

(5)Without prejudice to section 82(3), regulations under this section may fix or provide for the determination of different fees in relation to different functions, or in relation to the same function in different circumstances.

(6)The power to make regulations under this section shall be exercisable—

(a)as regards functions with respect to matters not relating exclusively to agricultural operations, by the Secretary of State;

(b)as regards functions with respect to matters relating exclusively to the relevant agricultural purposes, by the appropriate argicultural authority.

(7)Regulations under this section as regards functions falling within subsection (6)(b) above may be either regulations applying to Great Britain and made by the Minister of Agriculture, Fisheries and Food and the Secretary of State acting jointly, or regulations applying to England and Wales only and made by the said Minister, or regulations applying to Scotland only and made by the Secretary of State; and in subsection (6)(b) above " the appropriate agricultural authority" shall be construed accordingly.

(8)In subsection (4) above the references to a person training for employment and a person seeking training for employment shall include respectively a person attending an industrial rehabilitation course provided by virtue of the [1973 c. 50.] Employment and Training Act 1973 and a person seeking to attend such a course.

(9)For the purposes of this section the performance by an inspector of his functions shall be treated as the performance by the enforcing authority which appointed him of functions conferred on that authority by or under any of the relevant statutory provisions.

Miscellaneous and supplementary

44Appeals in connection with licensing provisions in the relevant statutory provisions

(1)Any person who is aggrieved by a decision of an authority having power to issue licences (other than agricultural licences and nuclear site licences) under any of the relevant statutory provisions—

(a)refusing to issue him a licence, to renew a licence held by him, or to transfer to him a licence held by another;

(b)issuing him a licence on or subject to any term, condition or restriction whereby he is aggrieved ;

(c)varying or refusing to vary any term, condition or restriction on or subject to which a licence is held by him; or

(d)revoking a licence held by him,

may appeal to the Secretary of State.

(2)The Secretary of State may, in such cases as he considers it appropriate to do so, having regard to the nature of the questions which appear to him to arise, direct that an appeal under this section shall be determined on his behalf by a person appointed by him for that purpose.

(3)Before the determination of an appeal the Secretary of State shall ask the appellant and the authority against whose decision the appeal is brought whether they wish to appear and be heard on the appeal and—

(a)the appeal may be determined without a hearing of the parties if both of them express a wish not to appear and be heard as aforesaid ;

(b)the Secretary of State shall, if either of the parties expresses a wish to appear and be heard, afford to both of them an opportunity of so doing.

(4)The [1971 c. 62.] Tribunals and Inquiries Act 1971 shall apply to a hearing held by a person appointed in pursuance of subsection (2) above to determine an appeal as it applies to a statutory inquiry held by the Secretary of State, but as if in section 12(1) of that Act (statement of reasons for decisions) the reference to any decision taken by the Secretary of State included a reference to a decision taken on his behalf by that person.

(5)A person who determines an appeal under this section on behalf of the Secretary of State and the Secretary of State, if he determines such an appeal, may give such directions as he considers appropriate to give effect to his determination.

(6)The Secretary of State may pay to any person appointed to hear or determine an appeal under this section on his behalf such remuneration and allowances as the Secretary of State may with the approval of the Minister for the Civil Service determine.

(7)In this section—

(a)" licence " means a licence under any of the relevant statutory provisions other than an agricultural licence or nuclear site licence ;

(b)" nuclear site licence " means a licence to use a site for the purpose of installing or operating a nuclear installation within the meaning of the following subsection.

(8)For the purposes of the preceding subsection "nuclear installation " means—

(a)a nuclear reactor (other than such a reactor comprised in a means of transport, whether by land, water or air); or

(b)any other installation of such class or description as may be prescribed for the purposes of this paragraph or section 1(1)(b) of the [1965 c. 57.] Nuclear Installations Act 1965, being an installation designed or adapted for—

(i)the production or use of atomic energy ; or

(ii)the carrying out of any process which is preparatory or ancillary to the production or use of atomic energy and which involves or is capable of causing the emission of ionising radiations; or

(iii)the storage, processing or disposal of nuclear fuel or of bulk quantities of other radioactive matter, being matter which has been produced or irradiated in the course of the production or use of nuclear fuel;

and in this subsection—

- " atomic energy " has the meaning assigned by the [1946 c. 80.] Atomic Energy Act 1946 ;

- " nuclear reactor " means any plant (including any machinery, equipment or appliance, whether affixed to land or not) designed or adapted for the production of atomic energy by a fission process in which a controlled chain reaction can be maintained without an additional source of neutrons.

45Default powers

(1)Where, in the case of a local authority who are an enforcing authority, the Commission is of the opinion that an investigation should be made as to whether that local authority have failed to perform any of their enforcement functions, the Commission may make a report to the Secretary of State.

(2)The Secretary of State may, after considering a report submitted to him under the preceding subsection, cause a local inquiry to be held; and the provisions of subsections (2) to (5) of section 250 of the [1972 c. 70.] Local Government Act 1972 as to local inquiries shall, without prejudice to the generality of subsection (1) of that section, apply to a local inquiry so held as they apply to a local inquiry held in pursuance of that section.

(3)If the Secretary of State is satisfied, after having caused a local inquiry to be held into the matter, that a local authority have failed to perform any of their enforcement functions, he may make an order declaring the authority to be in default.

(4)An order made by virtue of the preceding subsection which declares an authority to be in default may, for the purpose of remedying the default, direct the authority (hereafter in this section referred to as " the defaulting authority ") to perform such of their enforcement functions as are specified in the order in such manner as may be so specified and may specify the time or times within which those functions are to be performed by the authority.

(5)If the defaulting authority fail to comply with any direction contained in such an order the Secretary of State may, instead of enforcing the order by mandamus, make an order transferring to the Executive such of the enforcement functions of the defaulting authority as he thinks fit.

(6)Where any enforcement functions of the defaulting authority are transferred in pursuance of the preceding subsection, the amount of any expenses which the Executive certifies were incurred by it in performing those functions shall on demand be paid to it by the defaulting authority.

(7)Any expenses which in pursuance of the preceding subsection are required to be paid by the defaulting authority in respect of any enforcement functions transferred in pursuance of this section shall be defrayed by the authority in the like manner, and shall be debited to the like account, as if the enforcement functions had not been transferred and the expenses had been incurred by the authority in performing them.

(8)Where the defaulting authority are required to defray any such expenses the authority shall have the like powers for the purpose of raising the money for defraying those expenses as they would have had for the purpose of raising money required for defraying expenses incurred for the purpose of the enforcement functions in question.

(9)An order transferring any enforcement functions of the defaulting authority in pursuance of subsection (5) above may provide for the transfer to the Executive of such of the rights, liabilities and obligations of the authority as the Secretary of State considers appropriate ; and where such an order is revoked the Secretary of State may, by the revoking order or a subsequent order, make such provision as he considers appropriate with respect to any rights, liabilities and obligations held by the Executive for the purposes of the transferred enforcement functions.

(10)The Secretary of State may by order vary or revoke any order previously made by him in pursuance of this section.

(11)In this section "enforcement functions", in relation to a local authority, means the functions of the authority as an enforcing authority.

(12)In the application of this section to Scotland—

(a)in subsection (2) for the words " subsections (2) to (5) of section 250 of the [1972 c. 70.] Local Government Act 1972 " there shall be substituted the words " subsections (2) to (8) of section 210 of the [1973 c. 65.] Local Government (Scotland) Act 1973 ", except that before 16th May 1975 for the said words there shall be substituted the words " subsections (2) to (9) of section 355 of the [1947 c. 43.] Local Government (Scotland) Act 1947 ";

(b)in subsection (5) the words "instead of enforcing the order by mandamus " shall be omitted.

46Service of notices

(1)Any notice required or authorised by any of the relevant statutory provisions to be served on or given to an inspector may be served or given by delivering it to him or by leaving it at, or sending it by post to, his office.

(2)Any such notice required or authorised to be served on or given to a person other than an inspector may be served or given by delivering it to him, or by leaving it at his proper address, or by sending it by post to him at that address.

(3)Any such notice may—

(a)in the case of a body corporate, be served on or given to the secretary or clerk of that body;

(b)in the case of a partnership, be served on or given to a partner or a person having the control or management of the partnership business or, in Scotland, the firm.

(4)For the purposes of this section and of section 26 of the [1889 c. 63.] Interpretation Act 1889 (service of documents by post) in its application to this section, the proper address of any person on or to whom any such notice is to be served or given shall be his last known address, except that—

(a)in the case of a body corporate or their secretary or clerk, it shall be the address of the registered or principal office of that body;

(b)in the case of a partnership or a person having the control or the management of the partnership business, it shall be the principal office of the partnership;

and for the purposes of this subsection the principal office of a company registered outside the United Kingdom or of a partnership carrying on business outside the United Kingdom shall be their principal office within the United Kingdom.

(5)If the person to be served with or given any such notice has specified an address within the United Kingdom other than his proper address within the meaning of subsection (4) above as the one at which he or someone on his behalf will accept notices of the same description as that notice, that address shall also be treated for the purposes of this section and section 26 of the [1889 c. 63.] Interpretation Act 1889 as his proper address.

(6)Without prejudice to any other provision of this section, any such notice required or authorised to be served on or given to the owner or occupier of any premises (whether a body corporate or not) may be served or given by sending it by post to him at those premises, or by addressing it by name to the person on or to whom it is to be served or given and delivering it to some responsible person who is or appears to be resident or employed in the premises.

(7)If the name or the address of any owner or occupier of premises on or to whom any such notice as aforesaid is to be served or given cannot after reasonable inquiry be ascertained, the notice may be served or given by addressing it to the person on or to whom it is to be served or given by the description of " owner" or " occupier" of the premises (describing them) to which the notice relates, and by delivering it to some responsible person who is or appears to be resident or employed in the premises, or, if there is no such person to whom it can be delivered, by affixing it or a copy of it to some conspicuous part of the premises.

(8)The preceding provisions of this section shall apply to the sending or giving of a document as they apply to the giving of a notice.

47Civil liability

(1)Nothing in this Part shall be construed—

(a)as conferring a right of action in any civil proceedings in respect of any failure to comply with any duty imposed by sections 2 to 7 or any contravention of section 8; or

(b)as affecting the extent (if any) to which breach of a duty imposed by any of the existing statutory provisions is actionable; or (c)as affecting the operation of section 12 of the [1965 c. 57.] Nuclear Installations Act 1965 (right to compensation by virtue of certain provisions of that Act).

(2)Breach of a duty imposed by health and safety regulations or agricultural health and safety regulations shall, so far as it causes damage, be actionable except in so far as the regulations provide otherwise.

(3)No provision made by virtue of section 15(6)(b) shall afford a defence in any civil proceedings, whether brought by virtue of subsection (2) above or not; but as regards any duty imposed as mentioned in subsection (2) above health and safety regulations or, as the case may be, agricultural health and safety regulations may provide for any defence specified in the regulations to be available in any action for breach of that duty.

(4)Subsections (1)(a) and (2) above are without prejudice to any right of action which exists apart from the provisions of this Act, and subsection (3) above is without prejudice to any defence which may be available apart from the provisions of the regulations there mentioned.

(5)Any term of an agreement which purports to exclude or restrict the operation of subsection (2) above, or any liability arising by virtue of that subsection shall be void, except in so far as health and safety regulations or, as the case may be, agricultural health and safety regulations provide otherwise.

(6)In this section " damage" includes the death of, or injury to, any person (including any disease and any impairment of a person's physical or mental condition).

48Application to Crown

(1)Subject to the provisions of this section, the provisions of this Part, except sections 21 to 25 and 33 to 42, and of regulations made under this Part shall bind the Crown.

(2)Although they do not bind the Crown, sections 33 to 42 shall apply to persons in the public service of the Crown as they apply to other persons.

(3)For the purposes of this Part and regulations made thereunder persons in the service of the Crown shall be treated as employees of the Crown whether or not they would be so treated apart from this subsection.

(4)Without prejudice to section 15(5), the Secretary of State may, to the extent that it appears to him requisite or expedient to do so in the interests of the safety of the State or the safe custody of persons lawfully detained, by order exempt the Crown either generally or in particular respects from all or any of the provisions of this Part which would, by virtue of subsection (1) above, bind the Crown.

(5)The power to make orders under this section shall be exercisable by statutory instrument, and any such order may be varied or revoked by a subsequent order.

(6)Nothing in this section shall authorise proceedings to be brought against Her Majesty in her private capacity, and this subsection shall be construed as if section 38(3) of the [1947 c. 44.] Crown Proceedings Act 1947 (interpretation of references in that Act to Her Majesty in her private capacity) were contained in this Act.

49Adaptation of enactments to metric units or appropriate metric units

(1)The appropriate Minister may by regulations amend—

(a)any of the relevant statutory provisions ; or

(b)any provision of an enactment which relates to any matter relevant to any of the general purposes of this Part but is not among the relevant statutory provisions ; or

(c)any provision of an instrument made or having effect under any such enactment as is mentioned in the preceding paragraph, by substituting an amount or quantity expressed in metric units for an amount or quantity not so expressed or by substituting an amount or quantity expressed in metric units of a description specified in the regulations for an amount or quantity expressed in metric units of a different description.

(2)The amendments shall be such as to preserve the effect of the provisions mentioned except to such extent as in the opinion of the appropriate Minister is necessary to obtain amounts expressed in convenient and suitable terms.

(3)Regulations made by the appropriate Minister under this subsection may, in the case of a provision which falls within any of paragraphs (a) to (c) of subsection (1) above and contains words which refer to units other than metric units, repeal those words if the appropriate Minister is of the opinion that those words could be omitted without altering the effect of that provision.

(4)In this section the appropriate Minister means—

(a)in relation to any provision not relating exclusively to agricultural operations the Secretary of State ;

(b)in relation to any provision relating exclusively to the relevant agricultural purposes that applies to Great Britain or the United Kingdom the Agriculture Ministers;

(c)in relation to any provision so relating that applies to England and Wales only, the Minister of Agriculture, Fisheries and Food;

(d)in relation to any provision so relating that applies to Scotland only, the Secretary of State.

50Regulations under relevant statutory provisions

(1)Subject to subsection (5) below any power to make regulations conferred on the Secretary of State by any of the relevant statutory provisions may be exercised by him either so as to give effect (with or without modifications) to proposals for the making of regulations by him under that power submitted to him by the Commission or independently of any such proposals, but before making any regulations under any of those provisions independently of any such proposals the Secretary of State shall consult the Commission and such other bodies as appear to him to be appropriate.

(2)Where the Secretary of State proposes to exercise any such power as is mentioned in the preceding subsection so as to give effect to any such proposals as are there mentioned with modifications, he shall, before making the regulations, consult the Commission.

(3)Where the Commission proposes to submit to the Secretary of State any such proposals as are mentioned in subsection (1) above except proposals for the making of regulations under section 43(2), it shall, before so submitting them, consult—

(a)any government department or other body that appears to the Commission to be appropriate (and, in particular, in the case of proposals for the making of regulations under section 18(2), any body representing local authorities that so appears, and, in the case of proposals for the making of regulations relating to electro-magnetic radiations, the National Radiological Protection Board);

(b)such government departments and other bodies, if any, as, in relation to any matter dealt with in the proposals, the Commission is required to consult under this subsection by virtue of directions given to it by the Secretary of State.

(4)Where the Minister of Agriculture, Fisheries and Food and the Secretary of State or either of them propose or proposes to make any regulations under any of the relevant statutory provisions, they or he shall before making the regulations consult the Commission and such other bodies as appear to them or him to be appropriate.

(5)Subsections (1) to (3) above shall not apply to any power of the Secretary of State to make regulations which is capable of being exercised by him for Great Britain jointly with the Minister of Agriculture, Fisheries and Food.

51Exclusion of application to domestic employment

Nothing in this Part shall apply in relation to a person by reason only that he employs another, or is himself employed, as a domestic servant in a private household.

52Meaning of work and at work

(1)For the purposes of this Part—

(a)" work" means work as an employee or as a self-employed person;

(b)an employee is at work throughout the time when he is in the course of his employment, but not otherwise ; and

(c)a self-employed person is at work throughout such time as he devotes to work as a self-employed person;

and, subject to the following subsection, the expressions " work " and " at work", in whatever context, shall be construed accordingly.

(2)Regulations made under this subsection may—

(a)extend the meaning of " work " and " at work " for the purposes of this Part; and

(b)in that connection provide for any of the relevant statutory provisions to have effect subject to such adaptations as may be specified in the regulations.

(3)The power to make regulations under subsection (2) above shall be exercisable—

(a)in relation to activities not relating exclusively to agricultural operations, by the Secretary of State;

(b)in relation to activities relating exclusively to the relevant agricultural purposes, by the appropriate agriculture authority.

(4)Regulations under subsection (2) above in relation to activities falling within subsection (3)(b) above may be either regulations applying to Great Britain and made by the Minister of Agriculture, Fisheries and Food and the Secretary of State acting jointly, or regulations applying to England and Wales only and made by the said Minister, or regulations applying to Scotland only and made by the Secretary of State; and in subsection (3)(b) above " the appropriate agriculture authority " shall be construed accordingly.

53General interpretation of Part I

(1)In this Part, unless the context otherwise requires—

- " agriculture ", subject to subsection (3) below, includes horticulture, fruit growing, seed growing, dairy farming, livestock breeding and keeping (including the management of livestock up to the point of slaughter or export from Great Britain), forestry, the use of land as grazing land, meadow land, osier land, market gardens and nursery grounds, and the preparation of land for agricultural use, and " agricultural " shall be construed accordingly;

- " the Agriculture Ministers " means the Minister of Agriculture, Fisheries and Food and the Secretary of State and, in the case of anything falling to be done by the Agriculture Ministers, means those Ministers acting jointly;

- " agricultural health and safety regulations " has the meaning assigned by section 30(1);

- " agricultural licence " means a licence of the Agriculture Ministers or either of them under any of the relevant statutory provisions;

- " agricultural operation " does not include an agricultural operation performed otherwise than in the course of a trade, business or other undertaking (whether carried on for profit or not) but, subject to

193

subsection (2) below, includes any operation incidental to agriculture which is performed in the course of such a trade, business or undertaking;

- " the appropriate Agriculture Minister " means, for the purpose of the application of any of the relevant statutory provisions to England and Wales, the Minister of Agriculture, Fisheries and Food, and, for the purpose of the application of any of those provisions to Scotland, the Secretary of State ;

- " article for use at work " means—

(a)

any plant designed for use or operation (whether exclusively or not) by persons at work, and

(b)

any article designed for use as a component in any such plant;

- " code of practice" (without prejudice to section 16(8)) includes a standard, a specification and any other documentary form of practical guidance;

- " the Commission " has the meaning assigned by section 10(2);

- " conditional sale agreement " means an agreement for the sale of goods under which the purchase price or part of it is payable by instalments, and the property in the goods is to remain in the seller (notwithstanding that the buyer is to be in possession of the goods) until such conditions as to the payment of instalments or otherwise as may be specified in the agreement are fulfilled;

- " contract of employment " means a contract of employment or apprenticeship (whether express or implied and, if express, whether oral or in writing);

- " credit-sale agreement " means an agreement for the sale of goods, under which the purchase price or part of it is payable by instalments, but which is not a conditional sale agreement;

- " domestic premises " means premises occupied as a private dwelling (including any garden, yard, garage, outhouse or other appurtenance of such premises which is not used in common by the occupants of more than one such dwelling), and " non-domestic premises " shall be construed accordingly;

- " employee" means an individual who works under a contract of employment, and related expressions shall be construed accordingly;

- " enforcing authority " has the meaning assigned by section 18(7);

- " the Executive " has the meaning assigned by section 10(5);

- " the existing statutory provisions " means the following provisions while and to the extent that they remain in force, namely the provisions of the Acts mentioned in Schedule 1 which are specified in the third column of that Schedule and of the regulations, orders or other instruments of a legislative character made or having effect under any provision so specified ;

- " forestry " includes—

(a)

the felling of trees and the extraction and primary conversion of trees within the wood or forest in which they were grown, and

(b)

the use of land for woodlands where that use is ancillary to the use of land for other agricultural purposes;

- " the general purposes of this Part " has the meaning assigned by section 1;

- " health and safety regulations " has the meaning assigned by section 15(1);

- " hire-purchase agreement " means an agreement other than a conditional sale agreement, under which—

    (a)

goods are bailed or (in Scotland) hired in return for periodical payments by the person to whom they are bailed or hired ; and

    (b)

the property in the goods will pass to that person if the terms of the agreement are complied with and one or more of the following occurs:

    (i)

the exercise of an option to purchase by that person;

    (ii)

the doing of any other specified act by any party to the agreement;

    (iii)

the happening of any other event; and " hire-purchase " shall be construed accordingly ;

- " improvement notice " means a notice under section 21;

- " inspector " means an inspector appointed under section 19;

- " livestock " includes any creature kept for the production of food, wool, skins or fur, or for the purpose of its use in the carrying on of any agricultural activity;

- " local authority " means—

(a)

in relation to England and Wales, a county council, the Greater London Council, a district council, a London borough council, the Common Council of the City of London, the Sub-Treasurer of the Inner Temple or the Under-Treasurer of the Middle Temple,

(b)

in relation to Scotland, a regional, islands or district council except that before 16th May 1975 it means a town council or county council;

- " offshore installation " means any installation which is intended for underwater exploitation of mineral resources or exploration with a view to such exploitation ;

- "personal injury " includes any disease and any impairment of a person's physical or mental condition;

- " plant " includes any machinery, equipment or appliance ;

- " premises " includes any place and, in particular, includes—

(a)

any vehicle, vessel, aircraft or hovercraft,

(b)

any installation on land (including the foreshore and other land intermittently covered by water), any offshore installation, and any other installation (whether floating, or resting on the seabed or the subsoil thereof, or resting on other land covered with water or the subsoil thereof), and

(c)

any tent or movable structure ;

- " prescribed " means prescribed by regulations made by the Secretary of State;

- " prohibition notice " means a notice under section 22 ;

- " the relevant agricultural purposes " means the following purposes, that is to say—

(a)

securing the health, safety and welfare at work of persons engaged in agricultural operations,

(b)

protecting persons other than persons so engaged against risks to health or safety arising out of or in connection with the activities at work of persons so engaged; and the reference in paragraph (b) above to the risks there mentioned shall be construed in accordance with section 1(3);

- " the relevant statutory provisions " means—

(a)

the provisions of this Part and of any health and safety regulations and agricultural health and safety regulations; and

(b)

the existing statutory provisions ;

- " self-employed person " means an individual who works for gain or reward otherwise than under a contract of employment, whether or not he himself employs others;

- " substance " means any natural or artificial substance, whether in solid or liquid form or in the form of a gas or vapour;

- " substance for use at work " means any substance intended for use (whether exclusively or not) by persons at work;

- " supply ", where the reference is to supplying articles or substances, means supplying them by way of sale, lease, hire or hire-purchase, whether as principal or agent for another.

(2)In determining in any particular case whether an operation is incidental to agriculture within the meaning of the definition of " agricultural operation" in the preceding subsection, regard shall be had to the magnitude of the operation and to the scale on which it is performed as well as to all other relevant circumstances.

(3)Provision may be made by order for directing that for the purposes of this Part any activity or operation specified in the order which would or would not otherwise be agriculture within the meaning of this Part shall be treated as not being or, as the case may be, being agriculture for those purposes.

(4)An order under subsection (3) above may be either an order applying to Great Britain and made by the Minister of Agriculture, Fisheries and Food and the Secretary of State acting jointly, or an order applying to England and Wales only and made by the said Minister, or an order applying to Scotland only and made by the Secretary of State.

(5)An order under subsection (3) above may be varied or revoked by a subsequent order thereunder made by the authority who made the original order.

(6)The power to make orders under subsection (3) above shall be exercisable by statutory instrument subject to annulment in pursuance of a resolution of either House of Parliament.

54Application of Part I to Isles of Scilly

This Part, in its application to the Isles of Stilly, shall apply as if those Isles were a local government area and the Council of those Isles were a local authority.

PART IITHE EMPLOYMENT MEDICAL ADVISORY SERVICE

55Functions of, and responsibility for maintaining, employment medical advisory service

(1)There shall continue to be an employment medical advisory service, which shall be maintained for the following purposes, that is to say—

(a)securing that the Secretary of State, the Health and Safety Commission, the Manpower Services Commission and others concerned with the health of employed persons or of persons seeking or training for employment can be kept informed of, and adequately advised on, matters of which they ought respectively to take cognisance concerning the safeguarding and improvement of the health of those persons;

(b)giving to employed persons and persons seeking or training for employment information and advice on health in relation to employment and training for employment;

(c)other purposes of the Secretary of State's functions relating to employment.

(2)The authority responsible for maintaining the said service shall be the Secretary of State; but if arrangements are made by the Secretary of State for that responsibility to be discharged on his behalf by the Health and Safety Commission or some other body, then, while those arrangements operate, the body so discharging that responsibility (and not the Secretary of State) shall be the authority responsible for maintaining that service.

(3)The authority for the time being responsible for maintaining the said service may also for the purposes mentioned in subsection (1) above, and for the purpose of assisting employment medical advisers in the performance of their functions, investigate or assist in, arrange for or make payments in respect of the investigation of problems arising in connection with any such matters as are so mentioned or otherwise in connection with the functions of employment medical advisers, and for the purpose of investigating or assisting in the investigation of such problems may provide and maintain such laboratories and other services as appear to the authority to be requisite.

(4)Any arrangements made by the Secretary of State in pursuance of subsection (2) above may be terminated by him at any time, but without prejudice to the making of other arrangements at any time in pursuance of that subsection (including arrangements which are to operate from the time when any previous arrangements so made cease to operate).

(5)Without prejudice to sections 11(4)(a) and 12(b), it shall be the duty of the Health and Safety Commission, if so directed by the Secretary of State, to enter into arrangements with him for the Commission to be responsible for maintaining the said service.

(6)In subsection (1) above—

(a)the reference to persons training for employment shall include persons attending industrial rehabilitation courses provided by virtue of the [1973 c. 50.] Employment and Training Act 1973 ; and

(b)the reference to persons (other than the Secretary of State and the Commissions there mentioned) concerned with the health of employed persons or of persons seeking or training for employment shall be taken to include organisations representing employers, employees and occupational health practitioners respectively.

56Functions of authority responsible for maintaining the service

(1)The authority for the time being responsible for maintaining the employment medical advisory service shall for the purpose of discharging that responsibility appoint persons to be employment medical advisers, and may for that purpose appoint such other officers and servants as it may determine, subject however to the requisite approval as to numbers, that is to say—

(a)where that authority is the Secretary of State, the approval of the Minister for the Civil Service;

(b)otherwise, the approval of the Secretary of State given with the consent of that Minister.

(2)A person shall not be qualified to be appointed, or to be, an employment medical adviser unless he is a fully registered medical practitioner.

(3)The authority for the time being responsible for maintaining the said service may determine the cases and circumstances in which the employment medical advisers or any of them are to perform the duties or exercise the powers conferred on employment medical advisers by or under this Act or otherwise.

(4)Where as a result of arrangements made in pursuance of section 55(2) the authority responsible for maintaining the said service changes, the change shall not invalidate any appointment previously made under subsection (1) above, and any such appointment subsisting when the change occurs shall thereafter have effect as if made by the new authority.

57Fees

(1)The Secretary of State may by regulations provide for such fees as may be fixed by or determined under the regulations to be payable for or in connection with the performance by the authority responsible for maintaining the employment medical advisory service of any function conferred for the purposes of that service on that authority by virtue of this Part or otherwise.

(2)For the purposes of this section, the performance by an employment medical adviser of his functions shall be treated as the performance by the authority responsible for maintaining the said service of functions conferred on that authority as mentioned in the preceding subsection.

(3)The provisions of subsections (4), (5) and (8) of section 43 shall apply in relation to regulations under this section with the modification that references to subsection (2) of that section shall be read as references to subsection (1) of this section.

(4)Where an authority other than the Secretary of State is responsible for maintaining the said service, the Secretary of State shall consult that authority before making any regulations under this section.

58Other financial provisions

(1)The authority for the time being responsible for maintaining the employment medical advisory service may pay—

(a)to employment medical advisers such salaries or such fees and travelling or other allowances; and

(b)to other persons called upon to give advice in connection with the execution of the authority's functions under this Part such travelling or other allowances or compensation for loss of remunerative time; and

(c)to persons attending for medical examinations conducted by, or in accordance with arrangements made by, employment medical advisers (including pathological, physiological and radiological tests and similar investigations so conducted) such travelling or subsistence allowances or such compensation for loss of earnings,

as the authority may, with the requisite approval, determine.

(2)For the purposes of the preceding subsection the requisite approval is—

(a)where the said authority is the Secretary of State, the approval of the Minister for the Civil Service ;

(b)otherwise, the approval of the Secretary of State given with the consent of that Minister.

(3)Where an authority other than the Secretary of State is responsible for maintaining the said service, it shall be the duty of the Secretary of State to pay to that authority such sums as are approved by the Treasury and as he considers appropriate for the purpose of enabling the authority to discharge that responsibility.

59Duty of responsible authority to keep accounts and to report

(1)It shall be the duty of the authority for the time being responsible for maintaining the employment medical advisory service—

(a)to keep, in relation to the maintenance of that service, proper accounts and proper records in relation to the accounts;

(b)to prepare in respect of each accounting year a statement of accounts relating to the maintenance of that service in such form as the Secretary of State may direct with the approval of the Treasury; and

(c)to send copies of the statement to the Secretary of State and the Comptroller and Auditor General before the end of the month of November next following the accounting year to which the statement relates.

(2)The Comptroller and Auditor General shall examine, certify and report on each statement received by him in pursuance of subsection (1) above and shall lay copies of each statement and of his report before each House of Parliament.

(3)It shall also be the duty of the authority responsible for maintaining the employment medical advisory service to make to the Secretary of State, as soon as possible after the end of each accounting year, a report on the discharge of its responsibilities in relation to that service during that year; and the Secretary of State shall lay before each House of Parliament a copy of each report made to him in pursuance of this subsection.

(4)Where as a result of arrangements made in pursuance of section 55(2) the authority responsible for maintaining the employment medical advisory service changes, the change shall not affect any duty imposed by this section on the body which was responsible for maintaining that service before the change.

(5)No duty imposed on the authority for the time being responsible for maintaining the employment medical advisory service by subsection (1) or (3) above shall fall on the Commission (which is subject to corresponding duties under Schedule 2) or on the Secretary of State.

(6)In this section " accounting year " means, except so far as the Secretary of State otherwise directs, the period of twelve months ending with 31st March in any year.

60Supplementary

(1)It shall be the duty of the Secretary of State to secure that each Area Health Authority arranges for one of its officers who is a fully registered medical practitioner to furnish, on the application of an employment medical adviser, such particulars of the school medical record of a person who has not attained the age of eighteen and such other information relating to his medical history as the adviser may reasonably require for the efficient performance of his functions; but no particulars or information about any person which may be furnished to an adviser in pursuance of this subsection shall (without the consent of that person) be disclosed by the adviser otherwise than for the efficient performance of his functions.

(2)In its application to Scotland the preceding subsection shall have effect with the substitution of the words " every Health Board arrange for one of their " for the words from " each " to " its ".

(3)The Secretary of State may by order made by statutory instrument subject to annulment in pursuance of a resolution of either House of Parliament modify the provisions of section 7(3) and (4) of the [1973 c. 50.] Employment and

Training Act 1973 (which require a person's period of continuous employment by a relevant body or in the civil service of the State to be treated, for the purposes of sections 1 and 2 of the [1972 c. 53.] Contracts of Employment Act 1972 and of certain provisions of the [1971 c. 72.] Industrial Relations Act 1971 affecting the right of an employee not to be unfairly dismissed, as increased by reference to previous periods of continuous employment by such a body or in that service) for the purpose of securing that employment as an employment medical adviser by an authority other than the Secretary of State is similarly treated for those purposes.

An order under this subsection may be varied or revoked by a subsequent order thereunder.

(4)References to the chief employment medical adviser or a deputy chief employment medical adviser in any provision of an enactment or instrument made under an enactment shall be read as references to a person appointed for the purposes of that provision by the authority responsible for maintaining the employment medical advisory service.

(5)The following provisions of the [1972 c. 28.] Employment Medical Advisory Service Act 1972 (which are superseded by the preceding provisions of this Part or rendered unnecessary by provisions contained in Part I), namely sections 1 and 6 and Schedule 1, shall cease to have effect; but—

(a)in so far as anything done under or by virtue of the said section 1 or Schedule 1 could have been done under or by virtue of a corresponding provision of Part I or this Part, it shall not be invalidated by the repeal of that section and Schedule by this Act but shall have effect as if done under or by virtue of that corresponding provision; and

(b)any order made under the said section 6 which is in force immediately before the repeal of that section by this Act shall remain in force notwithstanding that repeal, but may be revoked or varied by regulations under section 43(2) or 57, as if it were an instrument containing regulations made under section 43(2) or 57, as the case may require.

(6)Where any Act (whether passed before, or in the same Session as, this Act) or any document refers, either expressly or by implication, to or to any enactment contained in any of the provisions of the said Act of 1972 which are mentioned in the preceding subsection, the reference shall, except where the context otherwise requires, be construed as, or as including, a reference to the corresponding provision of this Act.

(7)Nothing in subsection (5) or (6) above shall be taken as prejudicing the operation of section 38 of the [1889 c. 63.] Interpretation Act 1889 (which relates to the effect of repeals).

PART III BUILDING REGULATIONS, AND [1959 C. 24.] AMENDMENT OF BUILDING (SCOTLAND) ACT 1959
61Amendments of enactments relating to building regulations

(1)For sections 61 and 62 of the 1936 Act (power to make building regulations, and their application to existing buildings) there shall be substituted the following sections—

"61Power to make building regulations

(1)Subject to the provisions of Part II of the [1961 c. 64.] Public Health Act 1961, the Secretary of State shall have power, for any of the purposes mentioned in subsection (2) below, to make regulations with respect to the design and construction of buildings and the provision of services, fittings and equipment in or in connection with buildings. Regulations under this subsection shall be known as building regulations.

(2)The purposes referred to in the preceding subsection are the following, that is to say—

(a)securing the health, safety, welfare and convenience of persons in or about buildings and of others who may be affected by buildings or matters connected with buildings;

(b)furthering the conservation of fuel and power; and

(c)preventing waste, undue consumption, misuse or contamination of water.

(3)Building regulations may—

(a)provide for particular requirements of the regulations to be deemed to be complied with where prescribed methods of construction, prescribed types of materials or other prescribed means are used in or in connection with buildings;

(b)be framed to any extent by reference to a document published by or on behalf of the Secretary of State or any other person or any body, or by reference to the approval or satisfaction of any prescribed person or body.

(4)Building regulations may include provision as to—

(a)the giving of notices ;

(b)the deposit of plans of proposed work or work already executed (including provision as to the number of copies to be deposited);

(c)the retention by local authorities of copies of plans deposited with them in accordance with the regulations;

(d)the inspection and testing of work;

(e)the taking of samples.

(5)Building regulations may exempt from all or any of the provisions of building regulations any prescribed class of buildings, services, fittings or equipment.

(6)The Secretary of State may by direction exempt from all or any of the provisions of building regulations any particular building or, as regards any particular location, buildings of any particular class thereat, and may in either case do so either unconditionally or subject to compliance with any conditions specified in the direction.

(7)A person who contravenes any condition specified in a direction given under the preceding subsection or permits any such condition to be contravened shall be liable to a fine not exceeding £400 and to a further fine not exceeding £50 for each day on which the offence continues after he is convicted.

(8)For the purposes of building regulations and of any direction given or instrument made with reference to building regulations, buildings may be classified by reference to size, description, design, purpose, location or any other characteristic whatsoever.

62Application of building regulations to existing buildings etc.

(1)Building regulations may be made with respect to—

(a)alterations and extensions of buildings and of services, fittings and equipment in or in connection with buildings;

(b)new services, fittings, or equipment provided in or in connection with buildings;

(c)buildings and services, fittings and equipment in or in connection with buildings, so far as affected by—

(i)alterations or extensions of buildings ; or

(ii)new, altered or extended services, fittings or equipment in or in connection with buildings;

(d)the whole of any building, together with any services, fittings or equipment provided in or in connection therewith, in respect of which there are or are proposed to be carried out any operations which by virtue of section 74(1)(c) of the Health and Safety at Work etc. Act 1974 constitute the construction of a building for the purposes of this section ;

(e)buildings or parts of buildings, together with any services, fittings or equipment provided in or in connection therewith, in cases where the purposes for which or the manner or circumstances in which a building or part of a building is used change or changes in a way that constitutes a material change of use of the building or part within the meaning of the expression ' material change of use' as defined for the purposes of this paragraph by building regulations.

(2)So far as they relate to matters mentioned in the preceding subsection, building regulations may be made to apply to or in connection with buildings erected before the date on which the regulations came into force but, except as aforesaid (and subject to section 65(2) of the Health and Safety at Work etc. Act 1974) shall not apply to buildings erected before that date.".

(2)Without prejudice to the generality of subsection (1) of section 61 of the 1936 Act as substituted by this section, building regulations may for any of the purposes mentioned in subsection (2) of that section make provision with respect to any of the matters mentioned in Schedule 5, may require things to be provided or done in or in connection with buildings (as well as regulating the provision or doing of things in or in connection with buildings), and may prescribe the manner in which work is to be carried out.

(3)The enactments relating to building regulations shall have effect subject to the further amendments provided for in Part I of Schedule 6.

(4)Section 65 of the 1936 Act and sections 4, 6 and 7 of the 1961 Act, as they will have effect after the coming into force of the preceding subsection, are set out in Part II of the said Schedule 6.

(5)Section 71 of the 1936 Act (exemption of certain buildings from building regulations) shall cease to have effect.

(6)Any regulations under section 4 of the 1961 Act which are in force immediately before the repeal of subsection (1) of that section by this Act shall not be invalidated by that repeal, but shall have effect as if made under section 61(1) of the 1936 Act as substituted by this section.

62 Further matters for which building regulations may provide

(1) Building regulations may make provision for requiring local authorities in such circumstances as may be prescribed to consult any prescribed person before taking any prescribed step in connection with any work or other matter to which building regulations are applicable.

(2) Building regulations—

(a) may authorise local authorities to accept, as evidence that the requirements of building regulations as to matters of any prescribed description are or would be satisfied, certificates to that effect by persons of any class or description prescribed in relation to those matters or by a person nominated in writing by the Secretary of State in any particular case ;

(b) may provide for the issue by local authorities of certificates to the effect that, so far as the authority concerned have been able to ascertain after taking all reasonable steps in that behalf, the requirements of building regulations as to matters of any prescribed description are satisfied in any particular case, and for such certificates to be evidence (but not conclusive evidence) of compliance with the regulations ;

(c) may make provision—

(i) for prohibiting, in prescribed circumstances, the carrying out of proposed work of any prescribed class involving matters of any prescribed description unless there has been deposited with the prescribed authority as regards those matters a certificate such as is mentioned in paragraph (a) above ;

(ii) for enabling, in cases where such a certificate is required by virtue of the preceding sub-paragraph, any dispute as to whether a certificate ought to be issued to be referred to the Secretary of State; and (iii)for enabling the Secretary of State, on any such reference, to give such directions as he thinks fit.

(3)Building regulations may authorise local authorities to charge prescribed fees for or in connection with the performance of prescribed functions of theirs relating to building regulations.

(4)Building regulations may make a prescribed person or class of persons responsible (instead of local authorities) for performing prescribed functions of local authorities under or in connection with building regulations, and for that purpose may provide for any prescribed enactment relating to building regulations and any prescribed provision of such regulations to apply (with any prescribed modifications) in relation to a prescribed person or a person of a prescribed class as that enactment or provision applies in relation to a local authority.

(5)Building regulations may repeal or modify any enactment to which this subsection applies if it appears to the Secretary of State that the enactment is inconsistent with, or is unnecessary or requires alteration in consequence of, any provision contained in or made under any enactment relating to building regulations.

This subsection applies to any enactment contained in this Act or in any other Act passed before or in the same Session as this Act, other than sections 61 to 71 of the 1936 Act, sections 4 to 11 of, and Schedule 1 to, the 1961 Act, and this Part.

63Miscellaneous provisions as to the approval of plans

(1)A local authority with whom plans of any proposed work are deposited in accordance with building regulations may in prescribed cases pass them by stages in accordance with the regulations and, where a local authority pass any such plans to a limited extent at any stage.—

(a)they shall impose conditions as to the depositing of further plans in connection with the proposed work; and

(b)they may impose conditions for securing that, pending the deposit of such of the further plans as they may indicate, the proposed work will not be proceeded with except to such extent as they may in accordance with the regulations authorise.

(2)A person who contravenes any condition imposed by a local authority under subsection (1) above other than a condition as to the depositing of further plans, or permits any such condition to be contravened, shall be liable to a fine not exceeding £400 and to a further fine not exceeding £50 for each day on which the offence continues after he is convicted.

(3)A local authority with whom plans of any proposed work are deposited in accordance with building regulations may, notwithstanding that the plans are defective or show that the work would contravene any of the building regulations, pass the plans provisionally, that is to say, subject to any modifications which they think necessary for remedying the defect or avoiding the contravention, indicating the modifications in the notice of approval and—

(a)if, within a prescribed time and in a prescribed manner so indicated, the person by or on behalf of whom the plans were deposited notifies the authority that he agrees to the modifications, the plans shall be treated as having been passed subject to those modifications; and

(b)if not, the plans shall be treated as having been rejected.

(4)In cases where by virtue of subsection (1) or (3) above plans are passed by stages or provisionally, the provisions of section 64(1) to (3) of the 1936 Act shall have effect subject to such modifications as may be prescribed.

(5)Where plans of any proposed work have been passed under section 64 of the 1936 Act by a local authority, the person by or on behalf of whom the plans were in accordance with building regulations deposited with the authority may, and in such cases as may be prescribed shall, for the purpose of obtaining the approval of the authority to any proposed departure or deviation from the plans as passed, deposit plans of any such departure or deviation ; and that section shall apply in relation to plans deposited under this subsection as it applies in relation to the plans originally deposited.

(6)Where in accordance with any existing enactment (however framed or worded) plans of a proposed building of any prescribed class are submitted to a Minister of the Crown for his approval—

(a)plans of the proposed building shall not be required to be deposited with the local authority for the purposes of section 64 of the 1936 Act in pursuance of building regulations;

(b)the Minister shall not approve the plans unless he is satisfied that, so far as applicable, the substantive requirements of building regulations will be complied with by and in connection with the proposed building;

(c)the approval of the plans by the Minister shall operate, for such purposes as may be prescribed, in the same way as the passing of them by the local authority would have operated;

(d)the Minister may exercise in connection with the proposed building the like powers of dispensing with or relaxing requirements of building regulations as are conferred on the Secretary of State and local authorities by virtue of section 6 of the 1961 Act (other than a power excepted by subsection (7) below), subject however to the like requirements as to consultation (if any) as apply by virtue of section 62(1) in the case of a local authority (but not to the requirements in the said section 6 as to consultation with the local authority) and to the like requirements as in the case of the Secretary of State apply by virtue of section 8 of the 1961 Act (opportunity to make representations about proposal to relax building regulations).

(7)In the preceding subsection " existing enactment" means an enactment passed before the coming into force of that subsection, other than an enactment relating to town and country planning; and the power excepted from paragraph (d) of that subsection is one which by virtue of section 62(4) is exercisable otherwise than by a local authority.

64Special provisions as to materials etc. unsuitable for permanent buildings

(1)This section applies—

(a)to any work consisting of a part of a building, being a part in the construction of which there is used any material or component of a type which, in relation to a part of that description, is prescribed for the purposes of this paragraph under subsection (2) below; and

(b)to any work provided in or in connection with a building, being work consisting of a service, fitting or item of equipment of a type so prescribed for the purposes of this paragraph.

(2)The Secretary of State may by building regulations—

(a)prescribe a type of material or component for the purposes of subsection (1)(a) above if in his opinion materials or components of that type are likely to be unsuitable for use in the construction of a particular part of a permanent building in the absence of conditions with respect to the use of the building or with respect to any material or component of that type used in the construction of a part of that description;

(b)prescribe a type of service, fitting or equipment for the purposes of subsection (1)(b) above if in his opinion services, fittings or equipment of that type are likely to be unsuitable for provision in or in connection with a permanent building in the absence of conditions with respect to the use of the building or with respect to any service, fitting or equipment of that type so provided.

215

(3)Where plans of any proposed work are, in accordance with building regulations, deposited with a local authority and the plans show that the proposed work would include or consist of work to which this section applies, the authority may, notwithstanding that the plans conform with the regulations—

(a)reject the plans ; or

(b)in passing the plans fix a period on the expiration of which the work to which this section applies or the relevant building (as the authority may in passing the plans direct) must be removed and, if they think fit, impose with respect to the use of the relevant building or with respect to the work to which this section applies such reasonable conditions, if any, as they consider appropriate, so however that no condition as to the use of the relevant building shall be imposed which conflicts with any condition imposed or having effect as if imposed under Part III or IV of the [1971 c. 78.] Town and Country Planning Act 1971.

(4)If, in the case of any work in respect of which plans ought by virtue of building regulations to have been deposited with a local authority but have not been so deposited, the work appears to the authority to include or consist of work to which this section applies, the authority, without prejudice to their right to take proceedings in respect of any contravention of the regulations, may fix a period on the expiration of which the work to which this section applies or the relevant building (as the authority may in fixing the period direct) must be removed and, if they think fit, impose any conditions that might have been imposed under the preceding subsection in passing plans for the first-mentioned work and, where they fix such a period, shall forthwith give notice thereof, and of any conditions imposed, to the owner of the relevant building.

(5)If, in the case of any work appearing to the local authority to fall within subsection (1)(b) above, plans of the work were not required by building regulations to be deposited with the authority, and were not so deposited, the authority may at any time within twelve months from the date of completion of the work fix a period on the expiration of which the work must be removed and, if they think fit, impose any conditions which, if plans of the work had been required to be, and had been, so deposited, might have been imposed under subsection (3) above in passing the plans and, where they fix such a period, shall forthwith give notice thereof, and of any conditions imposed, to the owner of the relevant building.

(6)A local authority may from time to time extend any period fixed, or vary any conditions imposed, under this section, but so that, unless an application in that behalf is made to them by the owner of the relevant building, they shall not exercise their power of varying conditions so imposed except when granting an extension or further extension of the period fixed with respect to the work or building, as the case may be.

(7)Any person aggrieved by the action of a local authority under this section in rejecting plans, or in fixing or refusing to extend any period, or in imposing or refusing to vary any conditions, may appeal to the Secretary of State within the prescribed time and in the prescribed manner.

(8)Where a period has been fixed under this section with respect to any work to which this section applies or with respect to the relevant building, the owner of that building shall on the expiration of that period or, as the case may be, of that period as extended, remove the work or building with respect to which the period was fixed ; and if he fails to do so, the local authority may remove that work or building, as the case may be, and may recover from him the expenses reasonably incurred by them in doing so.

(9)A person who—

(a)contravenes any condition imposed under this section or permits any such condition to be contravened; or

(b)contravenes subsection (8) above;

shall be liable to a fine not exceeding £400 and to a further fine not exceeding £50 for each day on which the offence continues or, as the case may be, on which the work or building is allowed to remain, after he is convicted; but this subsection shall not be construed as prejudicing a local authority's rights under subsection (8) above.

(10)In this section " the relevant building " means, in any particular case, the building mentioned in paragraph (a) or, as the case may be, paragraph (b) of subsection (1) above

(11)Section 53 of the 1936 Act (which is superseded by the preceding provisions of this section) shall cease to have effect, but—

(a)any building regulations made, period fixed, condition imposed or other thing done by virtue of that section shall be deemed to have been made, fixed, imposed or done by virtue of this section ; and

(b)anything begun under that section may be continued under this Act as if begun under this section, so however that any appeal under subsection (4) of that section which is pending at the time when that section ceases to have effect, and any proceedings arising out of such appeal, shall proceed as if that section were still in force.

65Continuing requirements

(1)Building regulations may impose on owners and occupiers of buildings to which building regulations are applicable such continuing requirements as the Secretary of State considers appropriate for securing, with respect to any provision of building regulations designated in the regulations as a provision to which those requirements relate, that the purposes of that provision are not frustrated; but a continuing requirement imposed by virtue of this subsection shall not apply in relation to a building unless a provision of building regulations so designated as one to which the requirement relates applies to that building.

(2)Building regulations may impose on owners and occupiers of buildings of any prescribed class (whenever erected, and whether or not any building regulations were applicable to them at the time of their erection) continuing requirements with respect to all or any of the following matters, namely—

(a)the conditions subject to which any services, fittings or equipment provided in or in connection with any building of that class may be used;

(b)the inspection and maintenance of any services, fittings or equipment so provided ; and

(c)the making of reports to any prescribed authority on the condition of any services, fittings or equipment so provided;

and so much of section 62 of the 1936 Act as restricts the application of building regulations shall not apply to regulations made by virtue of this subsection.

(3)If a person contravenes a continuing requirement imposed by virtue of this section, the local authority, without prejudice to their right to take proceedings for a fine in respect of the contravention, may execute any work or take any other action required to remedy the contravention, and may recover from that person the expenses reasonably incurred by them in so doing.

(4)Where a local authority have power under the preceding subsection to execute any work or take any other action they may, instead of exercising that power, by notice require the owner or the occupier of the building to which the contravention referred to in that subsection relates to execute that work or take that action.

The provisions of Part XII of the 1936 Act with respect to appeals against, and the enforcement of, notices requiring the execution of works shall apply in relation to any notice given under this section, subject however to the modification that in those provisions references to the execution of works shall be construed as references to the execution of work or the taking of other action, and references to work shall be construed accordingly.

(5)The provisions of sections 6, 7 and 8 of the 1961 Act (power to dispense with or relax requirements in building regulations, and related provisions) shall have effect in relation to continuing requirements imposed by virtue of this section subject to the following modifications, that is to say—

(a)a direction under the said section 6 shall, if it so provides, cease to have effect at the end of such period as may be specified in the direction ; and

(b)in subsection (1) of the said section 7 (as amended by this Act), the reference to granting an application subject to conditions shall be read as including a reference to granting an application for a limited period.

66Type relaxation of building regulations

(1)If the Secretary of State considers that the operation of any requirement of building regulations would be unreasonable in relation to any particular type of building matter, he may, either on an application made to him or of his own accord, give a direction dispensing with or relaxing that requirement generally in relation to that type of building matter, either unconditionally or subject to compliance with any conditions specified in the direction, being conditions with respect to matters directly connected with the dispensation or relaxation.

(2)A direction under subsection (1) above—

(a)shall, if it so provides, cease to have effect at the end of such period as may be specified in the direction;

(b)may be varied or revoked by a subsequent direction of the Secretary of State.

(3)Building regulations may require a person making an application under subsection (1) above to pay the Secretary of State the prescribed fee; and, without prejudice to section 4(2) of the 1961 Act, regulations made by virtue of this subsection may prescribe different fees for different cases:

Provided that the Secretary of State may in any particular case remit the whole or part of any fee payable by virtue of this subsection.

(4)Before giving a direction under this section the Secretary of State shall consult such bodies as appear to him to be representative of the interests concerned (including in particular, in the case of a direction that relates to a requirement relevant to any of their functions, the National Water Council).

(5)Where the Secretary of State gives a direction under this section, he shall publish notice of that fact in such manner as he thinks fit.

(6)A person who contravenes any condition specified in a direction given under this section or permits any such condition to be contravened shall be liable to a fine not exceeding £400 and to a further fine not exceeding £50 for each day on which the offence continues after he is convicted.

(7)If at any time a direction under subsection (1) above dispensing with or relaxing a requirement of building regulations ceases to have effect by virtue of subsection (2)(c) above or is varied or revoked under subsection (2)(b) above, mat fact shall not affect the continued operation of the direction (with any conditions specified therein) in any case in which before that time—

(a)plans of the proposed work were, in accordance with building regulations, deposited with a local authority; or

(b)a building notice was served on the district surveyor in pursuance of section 83 of the [1939 c. xcvii.] London Building Acts (Amendment) Act 1939.

(8)In this section and section 67 below " building matter " means any building or other matter whatsoever to which building regulations are in any circumstances applicable.

67Power of Secretary of State to approve types of building etc.

(1)The following provisions of this section shall have effect with a view to enabling the Secretary of State, either on an application made to him or of his own accord, to approve any particular type of building matter as complying, either generally or in any class of case, with particular requirements of building regulations.

(2)An application for the approval under this section of a type of building matter shall comply with any requirements of building regulations as to the form of such applications and the particulars to be included therein.

(3)Where under subsection (1) above the Secretary of State approves a type of building matter as complying with particular requirements of building regulations either generally or in any class of case, he may issue a certificate to that effect specifying—

(a)the type of building matter to which the certificate relates ;

(b)the requirements of building regulations to which the certificate relates; and

(c)where applicable, the class or classes of case to which the certificate applies.

(4)A certificate under this section shall, if it so provides, cease to have effect at the end of such period as may be specified in the certificate.

(5)If, while a certificate under this section is in force, it is found, in any particular case involving a building matter of the type to which the certificate relates, that the building matter in question is of that type and the case is one to which the certificate applies, that building matter shall in that particular case be deemed to comply with the requirements of building regulations to which the certificate relates.

(6)The Secretary of State may vary a certificate under this section either on an application made to him or of his own accord; but in the case of a certificate issued on an application made by a person under subsection (1) above, the

Secretary of State, except where he varies it on the application of that person, shall before varying it give that person reasonable notice that he proposes to do so.

(7)Building regulations may require a person making an application under subsection (1) or (6) above to pay the Secretary of State the prescribed fee ; and, without prejudice to section 4(2) of the 1961 Act, regulations made by virtue of this subsection may prescribe different fees for different cases:

Provided that the Secretary of State may in any particular case remit the whole or part of any fee payable by virtue of this subsection.

(8)The Secretary of State may revoke a certificate issued under this section, but before doing so in the case of a certificate issued on an application under subsection (1) above shall give the person on whose application the certificate was issued reasonable notice that he proposes to do so.

(9)Where the Secretary of State issues a certificate under this section or varies or revokes a certificate so issued, he shall publish notice of that fact in such manner as he thinks fit.

(10)If at any time a certificate under this section ceases to have effect by virtue of subsection (4) above or is varied or revoked under the preceding provisions of this section, that fact shall not affect the continued operation of subsection (5) above by virtue of that certificate in any case in which before that time—

(a)plans of the proposed work were, in accordance with building regulations, deposited with a local authority; or

(b)a building notice was served on the district surveyor in pursuance of section 83 of the [1939 c. xcvii.] London Building Acts (Amendment) Act 1939.

(11)For the purposes of subsection (3) above or any variation of a certificate under subsection (6) above, a class of case may be framed in any way that the Secretary of State thinks fit.

(12)The Secretary of State may by building regulations delegate to any person or body, to such extent and subject to such conditions as the Secretary of State may think fit, the powers of approval conferred on him by this section; and so far as those powers are for the time being so delegated to any person or body, the preceding provisions of this section, except so much of subsection (7) as precedes the proviso, and any building regulation made by virtue of that subsection shall (subject to any prescribed conditions) have effect in relation to that person or body with the substitution of references to that person or body for references to the Secretary of State.

68Power to require or carry out tests for conformity with building regulations

(1)The following subsection shall have effect for the purpose of enabling a local authority to ascertain, as regards any work or proposed work to which building regulations for the enforcement of which they are responsible are applicable, whether any provision of building regulations is or would be contravened by, or by anything done or proposed to be done in connection with, that work.

(2)The local authority shall have power for that purpose—

(a)to require any person by whom or on whose behalf the work was, is being or is proposed to be done to carry out such reasonable tests of or in connection with the work as may be specified in the requirement; or

(b)themselves to carry out any reasonable tests of or in connection with the work, and to take any samples necessary to enable them to carry out any such test.

(3)Without prejudice to the generality of the preceding subsection, the matters with respect to which tests may be required or carried out under that subsection include—

(a)tests of the soil or subsoil of the site of any building ;

(b)tests of any material, component or combination of components which has been, is being or is proposed to be used in the construction of a building, and tests of any service, fitting or equipment which has been, is being or is proposed to be provided in or in connection with a building.

(4)A local authority shall have power, for the purpose of ascertaining whether there is or has been, in the case of any building, any contravention of any continuing requirement that applies in relation to that building—

(a)to require the owner or occupier of the building to carry out such reasonable tests as may be specified in the requirement under this paragraph ; or

(b)themselves to carry out any tests which they have power to require under the preceding paragraph, and to take any samples necessary to enable them to carry out any such test. In this subsection " continuing requirement" means a continuing requirement imposed by building regulations made by virtue of section 65(1) or (2).

(5)The expense of carrying out any tests which a person is required to carry out under this section shall be met by that person:

Provided that the local authority, on an application made to them, may, if they think it reasonable to do so, direct that the expense of carrying out any such tests, or such part of that expense as may be specified in the direction, shall be met by the local authority.

(6)Any question arising under this section between a local authority and any person as to the reasonableness—

(a)of any test specified in a requirement imposed on him by the authority under this section ; or

(b)of a refusal by the authority to give a direction under subsection (5) above on an application made by him; or

(c)of a direction under that subsection given on such an application, may on the application of that person be determined by a court of summary jurisdiction ; and in a case falling within paragraph (b) or (c) above the court may order the expense to which the application relates to be met by the local authority to such extent as the court thinks just.

69Provisions relating to appeals etc. to the Secretary of State under certain provisions

(1)On an appeal to the Secretary of State under section 64 of the 1936 Act, section 7 of the 1961 Act or section 64 of this Act, the Secretary of State may at his discretion afford to the appellant and the local authority an opportunity of appearing before, and being heard by, a person appointed by the Secretary of State for the purpose.

(2)On determining any such appeal as is mentioned in subsection (1) above, the Secretary of State shall give such directions, if any, as he considers appropriate for giving effect to his determination.

(3)Where the Secretary of State gives a decision in proceedings—

(a)on any such appeal as is mentioned in subsection (1) above; or

(b)on a reference under section 67 of the 1936 Act; or

(c)on any application for a direction under section 6 of the 1961 Act where the power of giving the direction is not exercisable by the local authority,

the relevant person or the local authority may appeal to the High Court against the decision on a point of law.

In this subsection " the relevant person "—

(i)as regards such an appeal as is mentioned in paragraph (a) above, means the appellant;

(ii)as regards a reference under the said section 67, means the person on whose application (jointly with the local authority) the reference was made ;

(iii)as regards any such application as is mentioned in paragraph (c) above, means the applicant.

(4)At any stage of the proceedings on any such appeal, reference or application as is mentioned in the preceding subsection, the Secretary of State may state any question of law arising in the course of the proceedings in the form of a special case for the decision of the High Court; and a decision of the High Court on a case stated by virtue of this subsection shall be deemed to be a judgment of the court within the meaning of section 27 of the [1925 c. 49.] Supreme Court of Judicature (Consolidation) Act 1925 (jurisdiction of the Court of Appeal to hear and determine appeals from any judgment of the High Court).

(5)In relation to any proceedings in the High Court or the Court of Appeal brought by virtue of this section the power to make rules of court shall include power to make rules—

(a)prescribing the powers of the High Court or the Court of Appeal with respect to the remitting of the matter with the opinion or direction of the court for re-hearing and determination by the Secretary of State ; and

(b)providing for the Secretary of State, either generally or in such circumstances as may be prescribed by the rules, to be treated as a party to any such proceedings and to be entitled to appear and to be heard accordingly.

(6)Rules of court relating to any such proceedings as are mentioned in subsection (5) of this section may provide for excluding so much of section 63(1) of the said Act of 1925 as requires appeals to the High Court to be heard and determined by a Divisional Court; but no appeal to the Court of Appeal shall be brought by virtue of this section except with the leave of the High Court or the Court of Appeal.

(7)In this section " decision" includes a direction, and references to the giving of a decision shall be construed accordingly.

(8)Without prejudice to section 4(5) of the 1961 Act, building regulations may in connection with any such appeal as is mentioned in subsection (1) above include such supplementary provisions with respect to procedure as the Secretary of State thinks fit.

70 Power to make building regulations for Inner London

(1)The following enactments (which relate to the power to make, and other matters connected with, building regulations), namely sections 61, 62 and 67 of the 1936 Act and sections 4(2) and (5) to (7), 5 and 9 of the 1961 Act, shall (with this Part, except section 75 and Schedule 7) apply throughout Inner London as they apply elsewhere in England and Wales; but without prejudice to that power as extended by this subsection, this subsection shall not of itself cause any building regulations made before it comes into force to apply to Inner London.

(2)Subject to any provision made by virtue of section 62(4), it shall be the duty of the Greater London Council to enforce in Inner London any building regulations which are in force there except to the extent that other local authorities or district surveyors within the meaning of the London Building Acts 1930 to 1939 are by virtue of building regulations made responsible for their enforcement there.

(3)Where by virtue of this section or section 62(4) local authorities or any prescribed person or class of persons (other than local authorities) are made responsible for enforcing, or performing prescribed functions under or in connection with, building regulations in force in Inner London, then, without prejudice to the said section 62(4), building regulations may in that connection provide for any prescribed provision falling within section 76(1)(a) or (b) but not mentioned in subsection (1) above to apply (with any prescribed modifications, and notwithstanding paragraph 12 or 34 of Part I of Schedule 11 to the [1963 c. 33.] London Government Act 1963) in relation to any such authority or person, or persons of any such class, as that provision applies in relation to a local authority outside Inner London.

(4)Without prejudice to the generality of section 62(5) building regulations may repeal or modify any provision to which this subsection applies if it appears to the Secretary of State that the repeal or, as the case may be, the modification of that provision is expedient in consequence of the provisions of this section or in connection with any provision contained in building regulations that apply to or to any part of Inner London.

(5)The preceding subsection applies to any provision—

(a)of the London Building Acts 1930 to 1939 ;

(b)of any enactment contained in this Act, other than this Part, or in any other Act passed before or in the same Session as this Act, in so far as that provision—

(i)applies to or to any part of Inner London ; and

(ii)relates to, or to the making of, byelaws for or for any part of Inner London with respect to any matter for or in connection with which provision can be made by building regulations ;

(c)of any byelaws made or having effect under the said Acts or of any such byelaws as are mentioned in paragraph (b)(ii) above.

(6)Before making any building regulations that provide for the repeal or modification of any provision to which the preceding subsection applies, the Secretary of State shall (without prejudice to the requirements as to consultation in section 9(3) of the 1961 Act) consult the Greater London Council and any other local authority who appear to him to be concerned.

(7)In this section " Inner London" means the area comprising the Inner London boroughs, the City, and the Inner Temple and the Middle Temple.

(8)In Part I of Schedule 11 to the [1963 c. 33.] London Government Act 1963 (modifications of Public Health Acts)—

(a)in paragraph 12, for the words " 53 to 55, and 57 to 71 " there shall be substituted the words " 54, 55, 57 to 60, 64 to 66, 69, 70 and (so far as unrepealed) 71 ";

(b)in paragraph 34, for the words " 4 to 11" there shall be substituted the words " 4(3) and (4), 6 to 8 and 10 and (except in so far as it amends any enactment mentioned in section 70(1) of the Health and Safety at Work etc. Act 1974) section 11 ".

71Civil liability

(1)Subject to the provisions of this section, breach of a duty imposed by building regulations shall, so far as it causes damage, be actionable except in so far as the regulations provide otherwise ; and as regards any such duty building regulations may provide for any prescribed defence to be available in any action for breach of that duty brought by virtue of this subsection.

(2)Subsection (1) above and any defence provided for in regulations made by virtue thereof shall not apply in the case of a breach of such a duty in connection with a building erected before the date on which that subsection comes into force unless the regulations imposing the duty apply to or in connection with the building by virtue of section 62 of the 1936 Act or section 65(2) of this Act.

(3)Nothing in this section shall be construed as affecting the extent (if any) to which breach—

(a)of a duty imposed by or arising in connection with this Part or any other enactment relating to building regulations; or

(b)of a duty imposed by building regulations in a case to which subsection (1) above does not apply, is actionable, or as prejudicing any right of action which exists apart from the enactments relating to building regulations.

(4)In this section " damage " includes the death of, or injury to, any person (including any disease and any impairment of a person's physical or mental condition).

72Application to Crown

(1)Except in so far as building regulations provide otherwise, the substantive provisions of building regulations—

(a)shall apply in relation to work carried out or proposed to be carried out by or on behalf of a Crown authority (whether or not in relation to a Crown building) as they would apply if the person by or on behalf of whom the work was or is to be carried out were not a Crown authority; and

(b)so far as they consist of continuing requirements, shall apply to Crown authorities (whether or not in relation to Crown buildings) as they apply to persons who are not Crown authorities.

(2)In so far as building regulations so provide as regards any of the substantive requirements of building regulations, those requirements shall apply in relation to work carried out or proposed to be carried out as mentioned in subsection (1)(a) above in Inner London and, so far as they consist of continuing requirements, shall apply to Crown authorities there as mentioned in subsection (1)(b) above, even if those requirements do not apply there in the case of work carried out or proposed to be carried out otherwise than by or on behalf of a Crown authority or, in the case of continuing requirements, do not apply there to persons other than Crown authorities.

In this subsection " Inner London " has the same meaning as in section 70.

(3)Except in so far as building regulations provide otherwise, building regulations and the enactments relating to building regulations—

(a)shall apply in relation to work carried out or proposed to be carried out in relation to a Crown building otherwise than by or on behalf of a Crown authority, and, in the case of section 65 and building regulations made by virtue thereof, shall in relation to a Crown building apply to persons other than Crown authorities, as they would apply if the building were not a Crown building; and

(b)shall apply in relation to work carried out or proposed to be carried out by or on behalf of a government department acting for a person other than a Crown authority as they would apply if the work had been or were to be carried out by that person.

(4)Section 341 of the 1936 Act (power to apply provisions of that Act to Crown property) shall not apply to provisions relating to building regulations.

(5)Section 71 and any building regulations made by virtue of subsection (1) of that section shall apply in relation to duties imposed by building regulations in their application in accordance with the preceding provisions of this section.

(6)In the case of work carried out or proposed to be carried out by or on behalf of a Crown authority, and in any case in which a Crown authority is or (apart from any dispensation or relaxation) will be subject to any continuing requirements, that authority may exercise the like powers of dispensing with or relaxing the substantive requirements of building regulations or, as the case may be, the continuing requirements in question as are conferred on the Secretary of State and local authorities by virtue of section 6 of the 1961 Act (other than a power excepted by the following subsection), subject, however, to the like requirements as to consultation (if any) as apply by virtue of section 62(1) in the case of a local authority (but not the requirements of the said section 6 as to consultation with the local authority) and to the like requirements as in the case of the Secretary of State apply by virtue of section 8 of that Act (opportunity to make representations about proposal to relax building regulations); and no application shall be necessary for the exercise of any such powers by virtue of this subsection.

In relation to any continuing requirements references in this subsection to the said section 6 are references thereto as modified by section 65(5).

(7)The power excepted from the preceding subsection is one which by virtue of section 62(4) is exercisable otherwise than by a local authority.

(8)For the purposes of subsection (6) above work carried out or proposed to be carried out by or on behalf of a government department acting for another Crown authority shall be treated as carried out or proposed to be carried out by or on behalf of that department (and not by or on behalf of the other Crown authority).

(9)In this section—

- " continuing requirement " means a continuing requirement of building regulations imposed by virtue of section 65(1) or (2)(a) or (b).

- " Crown authority " means the Crown Estate Commissioners, a Minister of the Crown, a government department, any other person or body whose functions are performed on behalf of the Crown (not being a person or body whose functions are performed on behalf of Her Majesty in her private capacity), or any person acting in right of the Duchy of Lancaster or the Duchy of Cornwall;

- " Crown building " means a building in which there is a Crown interest or a Duchy interest;

- " Crown interest " means an interest belonging to Her Majesty in right of the Crown or belonging to a government department, or held in trust for Her Majesty for the purposes of a government department;

- " Duchy interest " means an interest belonging to Her Majesty in right of the Duchy of Lancaster, or belonging to the Duchy of Cornwall.

(10)If any question arises under this section as to which Crown authority is entitled to exercise any such powers as are mentioned in subsection (6) above, that question shall be referred to the Treasury, whose decision shall be final.

(11)The preceding provisions of this section shall, with any necessary modifications, apply in relation to the making of a material change in the use of a building within the meaning of building regulations made for the purposes of section 62(1)(e) of the 1936 Act (as substituted by this Part) as they apply in relation to the carrying out of work.

73Application to United Kingdom Atomic Energy Authority

(1)The provisions of section 72, except subsections (2) to (4), shall apply in relation to the United Kingdom Atomic Energy Authority (in this section referred to as " the Authority ") as if—

(a)the Authority were a Crown authority ;

(b)any building belonging to or occupied by the Authority were a Crown building; and

(c)the references in subsection (1) to not being a Crown authority were references to being neither a Crown authority nor the Authority,

but so that the said provisions shall not by virtue of this subsection apply in relation to dwelling-houses or offices belonging to or occupied by the Authority.

(2)Subject to the said provisions as applied by the preceding subsection, building regulations and the enactments relating to building regulations shall not apply in relation to buildings belonging to or occupied by the Authority, being buildings other than dwelling-houses or offices.

74Meaning of " building" etc. in connection with, and construction of references to, building regulations

(1)For the purposes of any enactment to which this subsection applies—

(a)" building " means any permanent or temporary building and, unless the context otherwise requires, includes any other structure or erection of whatever kind or nature (whether permanent or temporary), and in this paragraph, " structure or erection" shall include a vehicle, vessel, hovercraft, aircraft or other movable object of any kind in such circumstances as may be prescribed (being circumstances which in the opinion of the Secretary of State justify treating it for those purposes as a building);

(b)unless the context otherwise requires, any reference to a building includes a reference to part of a building, and any reference to the provision of services, fittings and equipment in or in connection with buildings, or to services, fittings and equipment so provided, includes a reference to the affixing of things to buildings or, as the case may be, to things so affixed ; and

(c)references to the construction or erection of a building shall include references to—

(i)the carrying out of such operations (whether for the reconstruction of a building, the roofing over of an open space between walls or buildings, or otherwise) as may be designated in building regulations as operations falling to be treated for those purposes as the construction or erection of a building, and

(ii)the conversion of a movable object into what is by virtue of paragraph (a) above a building,

and " construct" and " erect" shall be construed accordingly.

(2)The preceding subsection applies to sections 61 to 71 of the 1936 Act and to any other enactment (whether or not contained in the 1936 Act or this Act) which relates to building regulations or mentions " buildings " or " a building " in a context from which it appears that those expressions are there intended to have the same meaning as in the said sections 61 to 71.

(3)Unless the context otherwise requires, references in this Act or any other enactment (whether passed before or after this Act) to building regulations shall, in any particular case in relation to which any requirement of building regulations is for the time being dispensed with, waived, relaxed or modified by virtue of section 6 of the 1961 Act, section 66 of this Act or any other enactment, be construed as references to building regulations as they apply in that case.

75Amendment of Building (Scotland) Act 1959

The [1959 c. 24.] Building (Scotland) Act 1959 shall have effect subject to the amendments provided for in Schedule 7.

76Construction and interpretation of Part III and other provisions relating to building regulations

(1)The following provisions, namely—

(a)so much of Part II of the 1936 Act as relates to building regulations;

(b)so much of Part II of the 1961 Act as relates to building regulations; and

(c)this Part, except section 75 and Schedule 7 ;

shall be construed as one; and Part XII of the 1936 Act shall have effect as if the provisions mentioned in paragraph (b) and (c) above (as well as those mentioned in paragraph (a)) were contained in Part II of that Act.

(2)For the purposes of the provisions mentioned in subsection (1)(a) to (c) above—

(a)" local authority " means a district council, the Greater London Council, a London borough council, the Sub-Treasurer of the Inner Temple or the Under-Treasurer of the Middle Temple, and includes the Council of the Isles of Scilly; and (b)the definitions of " local authority" in section 1 (2) of the 1936 Act and section 2(3) of the 1961 Act shall not apply;

and in section 1(1) of the 1961 Act (Part II of that Act to be construed as one with Part II of the 1936 Act), after the words " Part II of this Act" there shall be inserted the words " , except so much of it as relates to building regulations, ".

(3)In this Part—

- " the 1936 Act " means the [1936 c. 49.] Public Health Act 1936;

- " the 1961 Act " means the [1961 c. 64.] Public Health Act 1961 ;

- " the substantive requirements of building regulations " means the requirements of building regulations with respect to the design and construction of buildings and the provision of services, fittings and equipment in or in connection with buildings (including requirements imposed by virtue of section 65(1) or (2)(a) or (b)), as distinct from procedural requirements.

(4)In this Part, in sections 61 to 71 of the 1936 Act and in sections 4 to 8 of the 1961 Act "prescribed" means prescribed by building regulations.

PART IVMISCELLANEOUS AND GENERAL
77Amendment of Radiological Protection Act 1970

(1)Section 1 of the [1970 c. 46.] Radiological Protection Act 1970 (establishment and functions of the National Radiological Protection Board) shall be amended in accordance with the following provisions of this subsection—

(a)after subsection (6) there shall be inserted as subsection (6A)—

"(6A)In carrying out such of their functions as relate to matters to which the functions of the Health and Safety Commission relate, the Board shall (without prejudice to subsection (7) below) act in consultation with the Commission and have regard to the Commission's policies with respect to such matters.";

(b)after subsection (7) there shall be inserted as subsections (7A) and (7B)—

"(7A)Without prejudice to subsection (6) or (7) above, it shall be the duty of the Board, if so directed by the Health Ministers, to enter into an agreement with the Health and Safety Commission for the Board to carry out on behalf of the Commission such of the Commission's functions relating to ionising or other radiations (including those which are not electro-magnetic) as may be determined by or in accordance with the direction; and the Board shall have power to carry out any agreement entered into in pursuance of a direction under this subsection.

(7B)The requirement as to consultation in subsection (7) above shall not apply to a direction under subsection (7A).";

(c)in subsection (8), after the words " subsection (7)" there shall be inserted the words " or (7A) ".

(2)In section 2(6) of the Radiological Protection Act 1970 (persons by whom, as regards premises occupied by the said Board, sections 1 to 51 of the [1963 c. 41.] Offices, Shops and Railway Premises Act 1963 and regulations thereunder are enforceable) for the words from " inspectors appointed " to the end of the subsection there shall be substituted the words " inspectors appointed by the Health and Safety Executive under section 19 of the Health and Safety at Work etc. Act 1974. "

78Amendment of Fire Precautions Act 1971

(1)The [1971 c. 40.] Fire Precautions Act 1971 shall be amended in accordance with the following provisions of this section.

(2)In section 1(2) (power to designate uses of premises for which fire certificate is compulsory) at the end there shall be inserted as paragraph if)—

"(f)use as a place of work."

(3)In section 2 (premises exempt from section 1), paragraphs (a) to (c) (which exempt certain premises covered by the [1963 c. 41.] Offices, Shops and Railway Premises Act 1963, the [1961 c. 34.] Factories Act 1961 or the [1954 c. 70.] Mines and Quarries Act 1954) shall cease to have effect.

(4)After section 9 there shall be inserted as section 9A—

"9ADuty to provide certain premises with means of escape in case of fire.

(1)All premises to which this section applies shall be provided with such means of escape in case of fire for the persons employed to work therein as may reasonably be required in the circumstances of the case.

(2)The premises to which this section applies are—

(a)office premises, shop premises and railway premises to which the Offices, Shops and Railway Premises Act 1963 applies; and

(b)premises which are deemed to be such premises for the purposes of that Act,

being (in each case) premises in which persons are employed to work.

(3)In determining, for the purposes of this section, what means of escape may reasonably be required in the case of any premises, regard shall be had (amongst other things) not only to the number of persons who may be expected to be working in the premises at any time but also to the number of persons (other than those employed to work therein) who may reasonably be expected to be resorting to the premises at that time.

(4)In the event of a contravention of subsection (1) above the occupier of the premises shall be guilty of an offence and liable on summary conviction to a fine not exceeding £400."

(5)In section 12(1) (power to make regulations about fire precautions as regards certain premises), at the end there shall be added the words " and nothing in this section shall confer on the Secretary of State power to make provision with respect to the taking or observance of special precautions in connection with the carrying on of any manufacturing process.

(6)In section 17 (duty of fire authorities to consult other authorities before requiring alterations to buildings)—

(a)in subsection (1), the word " and" shall be omitted where last occurring in paragraph (i) and shall be added at the end of paragraph (ii), and after paragraph

(ii)there shall be added as paragraph (iii)—

"(iii)if the premises are used as a place of work and are within the field of responsibility of one or more enforcing authorities within the meaning of Part I of the Health and Safety at Work etc. Act 1974, consult that authority or each of those authorities.";

(b)in subsection (2) (clarification of references in section 9 to persons aggrieved), for the words " or buildings authority" there shall be substituted the words " buildings authority or other authority ";

(c)after subsection (2) there shall be added as subsection (3)—

"(3)Section 18(7) of the Health and Safety at Work etc. Act 1974 (meaning in Part I of that Act of ' enforcing authority' and of such an authority's ' field of responsibility ') shall apply for the purposes of this section as it applies for the purposes of that Part."

(7)In section 18 (enforcement of Act)—

(a)for the word " it" there shall be substituted the words " (1) Subject to subsection (2) below, it ";

(b)for the word "section" there shall be substituted the word " subsection "; and

(c)after the word " offence " there shall be added as subsection (2)—

"(2)A fire authority shall have power to arrange with the Health and Safety Commission for such of the authority's functions under this Act as may be specified in the arrangements to be performed on their behalf by the Health and Safety Executive (with or without payment) in relation to any particular premises so specified which are used as a place of work."

(8)In section 40 (application to Crown etc.)—

(a)in subsection (1)(a) (provisions which apply to premises occupied by the Crown), after the word " 6 " there shall be inserted the words " , 9A (except subsection (4)) ";

(b)in subsection (1)(b) (provisions which apply to premises owned, but not occupied by, the Crown), after the word " 8 " there shall be inserted the word " 9A ";

(c)in subsection (10) (application of Act to hospital premises in Scotland), for the words from " Regional " to " hospitals" there shall be substituted the words " Health Board ";

(d)after subsection (10) there shall be inserted the following subsection—

"(10A)This Act shall apply to premises in England occupied by a Board of Governors of a teaching hospital (being a body for the time being specified in an order under section 15(1) of the [1973 c. 12.] National Health Service Reorganisation Act 1973) as if they were premises occupied by the Crown.".

(9)In section 43(1) (interpretation) there shall be added at the end the following definition—

- "" work " has the same meaning as it has for the purposes of Part I of the Health and Safety at Work etc. Act 1974".

(10)Schedule 8 (transitional provisions with respect to fire certificates under the [1961 c. 34.] Factories Act 1961 or the [1963 c. 41.] Offices, Shops and Railway Premises Act 1963) shall have effect.

79 Amendment of Companies Acts as to directors' reports

(1)The [1967 c. 81.] Companies Act 1967 shall be amended in accordance with the following provisions of this section.

(2)In section 16 (additional general matters to be dealt with in directors' reports) in subsection (1) there shall be added after paragraph (f)—

"(g)in the case of companies of such classes as may be prescribed by regulations made by the Secretary of State, contain such information as may be so prescribed about the arrangements in force in that year for securing the health, safety and welfare at work of employees of the company and its subsidiaries and for protecting other persons against risks to health or safety arising out of or in connection with the activities at work of those employees."

(3)After subsection (4) of the said section 16 there shall be added—

"(5)Regulations made under paragraph (g) of subsection (1) above may—

(a)make different provision in relation to companies of different classes;

(b)enable any requirements of the regulations to be dispensed with or modified in particular cases by any specified person or by any person authorised in that behalf by a specified authority ;

(c)contain such transitional provisions as the Secretary of State thinks necessary or expedient in connection with any provision made by the regulations.

(6)The power to make regulations under the said paragraph (g) shall be exercisable by statutory instrument which shall be subject to annulment in pursuance of a resolution of either House of Parliament.

(7)Any expression used in the said paragraph (g) and in Part I of the Health and Safety at Work etc. Act 1974 shall have the same meaning in that paragraph as it has in that Part of that Act and section 1(3) of that Act shall apply for interpreting that paragraph as it applies for interpreting that Part of that Act; and in subsection (5) above " specified" means specified in regulations made under that paragraph.".

80General power to repeal or modify Acts and instruments

(1)Regulations made under this subsection may repeal or modify any provision to which this subsection applies if it appears to the authority making the regulations that the repeal or, as the case may be, the modification of that provision is expedient in consequence of or in connection with any provision made by or under Part I.

(2)Subsection (1) above applies to any provision, not being among the relevant statutory provisions, which—

(a)is contained in this Act or in any other Act passed before or in the same Session as this Act; or

(b)is contained in any regulations, order or other instrument of a legislative character which was made under an Act before the passing of this Act; or

(c)applies, excludes or for any other purpose refers to any of the relevant statutory provisions and is contained in any Act not falling within paragraph (a) above or in any regulations, order or other instrument of a legislative character which is made under an Act but does not fall within paragraph (b) above.

(3)Without prejudice to the generality of subsection (1) above, the modifications which may be made by regulations thereunder include modifications relating to the enforcement of provisions to which this section applies (including the appointment of persons for the purpose of such enforcement, and the powers of persons so appointed).

(4)The power to make regulations under subsection (1) above shall be exercisable—

(a)in relation to provisions not relating exclusively to agricultural operations, by the Secretary of State ;

(b)in relation to provisions relating exclusively to the relevant agricultural purposes, by the appropriate agriculture authority;

but before making regulations under that subsection the Secretary of State or the appropriate agriculture authority shall consult such bodies as appear to the Secretary of State or, as the case may be, that authority to be appropriate.

(5)Regulations under subsection (1) above in relation to provisions falling within subsection (4)(b) above may be either regulations applying to Great Britain and made by the Minister of Agriculture, Fisheries and Food and the Secretary of State acting jointly, or regulations applying to England and Wales only and made by the said Minister, or regulations applying to Scotland only and made by the Secretary of State; and in subsection (4)(b) above " the appropriate agriculture authority " shall be construed accordingly.

(6)In this section " the relevant statutory provisions," " the relevant agricultural purposes " and " agricultural operation " have the same meaning as in Part I.

81Expenses and receipts

There shall be paid out of money provided by Parliament—

(a)any expenses incurred by a Minister of the Crown or government department for the purposes of this Act; and

(b)any increase attributable to the provisions of this Act in the sums payable under any other Act out of money so provided;

and any sums received by a Minister of the Crown or government department by virtue of this Act shall be paid into the Consolidated Fund.

82General provisions as to interpretation and regulations

(1)In this Act—

(a)" Act" includes a provisional order confirmed by an Act;

(b)" contravention" includes failure to comply, and "contravene" has a corresponding meaning;

(c)" modifications" includes additions, omissions and amendments, and related expressions shall be construed accordingly;

(d)any reference to a Part, section or Schedule not otherwise identified is a reference to that Part or section of, or Schedule to, this Act.

(2)Except in so far as the context otherwise requires, any reference in this Act to an enactment is a reference to it as amended, and includes a reference to it as applied, by or under any other enactment, including this Act.

(3)Any power conferred by Part I or II or this Part to make regulations—

(a)includes power to make different provision by the regulations for different circumstances or cases and to include in the regulations such incidental, supplemental and transitional provisions as the authority making the regulations considers appropriate in connection with the regulations; and

(b)shall be exercisable by statutory instrument, which shall be subject to annulment in pursuance of a resolution of either House of Parliament.

83Minor and consequential amendments, and repeals

(1)The enactments mentioned in Schedule 9 shall have effect subject to the amendments specified in that Schedule (being minor amendments or amendments consequential upon the provisions of this Act).

(2)The enactments mentioned in Schedule 10 are hereby repealed to the extent specified in the third column of that Schedule.

84Extent, and application of Act

(1)This Act, except—

(a)Part I and this Part so far as may be necessary to enable regulations under section 15 or 30 to be made and operate for the purpose mentioned in paragraph 2 of Schedule 3 ; and

(b)paragraphs 2 and 3 of Schedule 9,

does not extend to Northern Ireland.

(2)Part III, except section 75 and Schedule 7, does not extend to Scotland.

(3)Her Majesty may by Order in Council provide that the provisions of Parts I and II and this Part shall, to such extent and for such purposes as may be specified in the Order, apply (with or without modification) to or in relation to persons, premises, work, articles, substances and other matters (of whatever kind) outside Great Britain as those provisions apply within Great Britain or within a part of Great Britain so specified. For the purposes of this subsection " premises", " work " and " substance " have the same meaning as they have for the purposes of Part I.

(4)An Order in Council under subsection (3) above—

(a)may make different provision for different circumstances or cases;

(b)may (notwithstanding that this may affect individuals or bodies corporate outside the United Kingdom) provide for any of the provisions mentioned in that subsection, as applied by such an Order, to apply to individuals whether or not they are British subjects and to bodies corporate whether or not they are incorporated under the law of any part of the United Kingdom;

(c)may make provision for conferring jurisdiction on any court or class of courts specified in the Order with respect to offences under Part I committed outside Great Britain or with respect to causes of action arising by virtue of section 47(2) in respect of acts or omissions taking place outside Great Britain, and for the determination, in accordance with the law in force in such part of Great

Britain as may be specified in the Order, of questions arising out of such acts or omissions;

(d)may exclude from the operation of section 3 of the [1878 c. 73.] Territorial Waters Jurisdiction Act 1878 (consents required for prosecutions) proceedings for offences under any provision of Part I committed outside Great Britain;

(e)may be varied or revoked by a subsequent Order in Council under this section;

and any such Order shall be subject to annulment in pursuance of a resolution of either House of Parliament.

(5)In relation to proceedings for an offence under Part I committed outside Great Britain by virtue of an Order in Council under subsection (3) above, section 38 shall have effect as if the words " by an inspector, or " were omitted.

(6)Any jurisdiction conferred on any court under this section shall be without prejudice to any jurisdiction exercisable apart from this section by that or any other court.

85Short title and commencement

(1)This Act may be cited as the Health and Safety at Work etc. Act 1974.

(2)This Act shall come into operation on such day as the Secretary of State may by order made by statutory instrument appoint, and different days may be appointed under this subsection for different purposes.

(3)An order under this section may contain such transitional provisions and savings as appear to the Secretary of State to be necessary or expedient in connection with the provisions thereby brought into force, including such adaptations of those provisions or any provision of this Act then in force as appear to him to be necessary or expedient in consequence of the partial operation of this Act (whether before or after the day appointed by the order).

SCHEDULES

Sections 1 and 53.

SCHEDULE 1 EXISTING ENACTMENTS WHICH ARE RELEVANT STATUTORY PROVISIONS

Chapter	Short Title	Provisions which are relevant statutory provisions
1875 c. 17.	The Explosives Act 1875.	The whole Act except sections 30 to 32, 80 and 116 to 121.
1882 c. 22.	The Boiler Explosions Act 1882.	The whole Act.
1890 c. 35.	The Boiler Explosions Act 1890.	The whole Act.
1906 c. 14.	The Alkali, &c. Works Regulation Act 1906.	The whole Act.
1909 c. 43.	The Revenue Act 1909.	Section 11.
1919 c. 23.	The Anthrax Prevention Act 1919.	The whole Act.
1920 c. 65.	The Employment of Women, Young Persons and Children Act 1920.	The whole Act.
1922 c. 35.	The Celluloid and Cinematograph Film Act 1922.	The whole Act.
1923 c. 17.	The Explosives Act 1923.	The whole Act.

Chapter	Short Title	Provisions which are relevant statutory provisions
1926 c. 43.	The Public Health (Smoke Abatement) Act 1926.	The whole Act.
1928 c. 32.	The Petroleum (Consolidation') Act 1928	The whole Act.
1936 c. 22.	The Hours of Employment (Conventions) Act 1936.	The whole Act except section 5.
1936 c. 27.	The Petroleum (Transfer of Licences) Act 1936	The whole Act.
1937 c. 45.	The Hydrogen Cyanide (Fumigation) Act 1937.	The whole Act.
1945 c. 19.	The Ministry of Fuel and Power Act 1945.	Section 1(1) so far as it relates to maintaining and improving the safety, health and welfare of persons employed in or about mines and quarries in Great Britain.
1946 c. 59.	The Coal Industry Nationalisation Act 1946.	Section 42(1) and (2).
1948 c. 37.	The Radioactive Substances Act 1948.	Section 5(1)(a).

Chapter	Short Title	Provisions which are relevant statutory provisions
1951 c. 21.	The Alkali, &c. Works Regulation (Scotland) Act 1951.	The whole Act.
1951 c. 58.	The Fireworks Act 1951.	Sections 4 and 7.
1952 c. 60.	The Agriculture (Poisonous Substances) Act 1952.	The whole Act.
1953 c. 47.	The Emergency Laws (Miscellaneous Provisions) Act 1953.	Section 3.
1954 c. 70.	The Mines and Quarries Act 1954.	The whole Act except section 151.
1956 c. 49.	The Agriculture (Safety, Health and Welfare Provisions) Act 1956.	The whole Act.
1961 c. 34.	The Factories Act 1961.	The whole Act except section 135.
1961 c. 64.	The Public Health Act 1961.	Section 73.
1962 c. 58.	The Pipe-lines Act 1962.	Sections 20 to 26,33,34 and 42, Schedule 5.
1963 c. 41.	The Offices, Shops and Railway Premises Act 1963.	The whole Act.

Chapter	Short Title	Provisions which are relevant statutory provisions
1965 c. 57.	The Nuclear Installations Act 1965.	Sections 1, 3 to 6, 22 and 24, Schedule 2.
1969 c. 10.	The Mines and Quarries (Tips) Act 1969.	Sections 1 to 10.
1971 c. 20.	The Mines Management Act 1971.	The whole Act.
1972 c. 28.	The Employment Medical Advisory Service Act 1972.	The whole Act except sections 1 and 6 and Schedule 1.

Section 10.

SCHEDULE 2 ADDITIONAL PROVISIONS RELATING TO CONSTITUTION ETC. OF THE COMMISSION AND EXECUTIVE

Tenure of office

1 Subject to paragraphs 2 to 4 below, a person shall hold and vacate office as a member or as chairman or deputy chairman in accordance with the terms of the instrument appointing him to that office.

2 A person may at any time resign his office as a member or as chairman or deputy chairman by giving the Secretary of State a notice in writing signed by that person and stating that he resigns that office.

3(1) If a member becomes or ceases to be the chairman or deputy chairman, the Secretary of State may vary the terms of the instrument appointing him to be a member so as to alter the date on which he is to vacate office as a member.

(2)If the chairman or deputy chairman ceases to be a member he shall cease to be chairman or deputy chairman, as the case may be.

4(1)If the Secretary of State is satisfied that a member—

(a)has been absent from meetings of the Commission for a period longer than six consecutive months without the permission of the Commission ; or

(b)has become bankrupt or made an arrangement with his creditors; or

(c)is incapacitated by physical or mental illness ; or

(d)is otherwise unable or unfit to discharge the functions of a member,

the Secretary of State may declare his office as a member to be vacant and shall notify the declaration in such manner as the Secretary of State thinks fit; and thereupon the office shall become vacant.

(2)In the application of the preceding sub-paragraph to Scotland for the references in paragraph (b) to a member's having become bankrupt and to a member's having made an arrangement with his creditors there shall be substituted respectively references to sequestration of a member's estate having been awarded and to a member's having made a trust deed for behoof of his creditors or a composition contract.

Remuneration etc. of members

5The Commission may pay to each member such remuneration and allowances as the Secretary of State may determine.

6The Commission may pay or make provision for paying, to or in respect of any member, such sums by way of pension, superannuation allowances and gratuities as the Secretary of State may determine.

7Where a person ceases to be a member otherwise than on the expiry of his term of office and it appears to the Secretary of State that there are special circumstances which make it right for him to receive compensation, the

Commission may make to him a payment of such amount as the Secretary of State may determine.

Proceedings

8 The quorum of the Commission and the arrangements relating to meetings of the Commission shall be such as the Commission may determine.

9 The validity of any proceedings of the Commission shall not be affected by any vacancy among the members or by any defect in the appointment of a member.

Staff

10 It shall be the duty of the Executive to provide for the Commission such officers and servants as are requisite for the proper discharge of the Commission's functions; and any reference in this Act to an officer or servant of the Commission is a reference to an officer or servant provided for the Commission in pursuance of this paragraph.

11 The Executive may appoint such officers and servants as it may determine with the consent of the Secretary of State as to numbers and terms and conditions of service.

12 The Commission shall pay to the Minister for the Civil Service, at such times in each accounting year as may be determined by that Minister subject to any directions of the Treasury, sums of such amounts as he may so determine for the purposes of this paragraph as being equivalent to the increase during that year of such liabilities of his as are attributable to the provision of pensions, allowances or gratuities to or in respect of persons who are or have been in the service of the Executive in so far as that increase results from the service of those persons during that accounting year and to the expense to be incurred in administering those pensions, allowances or gratuities.

Performance of functions

13The Commission may authorise any member of the Commission or any officer or servant of the Commission or of the Executive to perform on behalf of the Commission such of the Commission's functions (including the function conferred on the Commission by this paragraph) as are specified in the authorisation.

Accounts and reports

14(1)It shall be the duty of the Commission—

(a)to keep proper accounts and proper records in relation to the accounts;

(b)to prepare in respect of each accounting year a statement of accounts in such form as the Secretary of State may direct with the approval of the Treasury; and

(c)to send copies of the statement to the Secretary of State and the Comptroller and Auditor General before the end of the month of November next following the accounting year to which the statement relates.

(2)The Comptroller and Auditor General shall examine, certify and report on each statement received by him in pursuance of this Schedule and shall lay copies of each statement and of his report before each House of Parliament.

15It shall be the duty of the Commission to make to the Secretary of State, as soon as possible after the end of each accounting year, a report on the performance of its functions during that year; and the Secretary of State shall lay before each House of Parliament a copy of each report made to him in pursuance of this paragraph.

Supplemental

16The Secretary of State shall not make a determination or give his consent in pursuance of paragraph 5, 6, 7 or 11 of this Schedule except with the approval of the Minister for the Civil Service.

17The fixing of the common seal of the Commission shall be authenticated by the signature of the secretary of the Commission or some other person authorised by the Commission to act for that purpose.

18A document purporting to be duly executed under the seal of the Commission shall be received in evidence and shall, unless the contrary is proved, be deemed to be so executed.

19In the preceding provisions of this Schedule—

(a)" accounting year " means the period of twelve months ending with 31st March in any year except that the first accounting year of the Commission shall, if the Secretary of State so directs, be such period shorter or longer than twelve months (but not longer than two years) as is specified in the direction ; and

(b)" the chairman ", " a deputy chairman " and " a member " mean respectively the chairman, a deputy chairman and a member of the Commission.

20(1)The preceding provisions of this Schedule (except paragraphs 10 to 12 and 15) shall have effect in relation to the Executive as if—

(a)for any reference to the Commission there were substituted a reference to the Executive ;

(b)for any reference to the Secretary of State in paragraphs 2 to 4 and 19 and the first such reference in paragraph 7 there were substituted a reference to the Commission;

(c)for any reference to the Secretary of State in paragraphs 5 to 7 (except the first such reference in paragraph 7) there were substituted a reference to the Commission acting with the consent of the Secretary of State ;

(d)for any reference to the chairman there were substituted a reference to the director, and any reference to the deputy chairman were omitted;

(e)in paragraph 14(1)(c) for the words from "Secretary" to " following " there were substituted the words " Commission by such date as the Commission may direct after the end of ".

(2)It shall be the duty of the Commission to include in or send with the copies of the statement sent by it as required by paragraph 14(1)(c) of this Schedule copies of the statement sent to it by the Executive in pursuance of the said paragraph 14(1)(c) as adapted by the preceding sub-paragraph.

(3)The terms of an instrument appointing a person to be a member of the Executive shall be such as the Commission may determine with the approval of the Secretary of State and the Minister for the Civil Service.

Section 15.

SCHEDULE 3 SUBJECT-MATTER OF HEALTH AND SAFETY REGULATIONS

1(1)Regulating or prohibiting—

(a)the manufacture, supply or use of any plant;

(b)the manufacture, supply, keeping or use of any substance;

(c)the carrying on of any process or the carrying out of any operation.

(2)Imposing requirements with respect to the design, construction, guarding, siting, installation, commissioning, examination, repair, maintenance, alteration, adjustment, dismantling, testing or inspection of any plant.

(3)Imposing requirements with respect to the marking of any plant or of any articles used or designed for use as components in any plant, and in that connection regulating or restricting the use of specified markings.

(4)Imposing requirements with respect to the testing, labelling or examination of any substance.

(5)Imposing requirements with respect to the carrying out of research in connection with any activity mentioned in sub-paragraphs (1) to (4) above.

2(1)Prohibiting the importation into the United Kingdom or the landing or unloading there of articles or substances of any specified description, whether absolutely or unless conditions imposed by or under the regulations are complied with.

(2)Specifying, in a case where an act or omission in relation to such an importation, landing or unloading as is mentioned in the preceding sub-paragraph constitutes an offence under a provision of this Act and of the [1952 c. 44.] Customs and Excise Act 1952, the Act under which the offence is to be punished.

3(1)Prohibiting or regulating the transport of articles or substances of any specified description.

(2)Imposing requirements with respect to the manner and means of transporting articles or substances of any specified description, including requirements with respect to the construction, testing and marking of containers and means of transport and the packaging and labelling of articles or substances in connection with their transport.

4(1)Prohibiting the carrying on of any specified activity or the doing of any specified thing except under the authority and in accordance with the terms and conditions of a licence, or except with the consent or approval of a specified authority.

(2)Providing for the grant, renewal, variation, transfer and revocation of licences (including the variation and revocation of conditions attached to licences).

5Requiring any person, premises or thing to be registered in any specified circumstances or as a condition of the carrying on of any specified activity or the doing of any specified thing.

6(1)Requiring, in specified circumstances, the appointment (whether in a specified capacity or not) of persons (or persons with specified qualifications or experience, or both) to perform specified functions, and imposing duties or conferring powers on persons appointed (whether in pursuance of the regulations or not) to perform specified functions.

(2)Restricting the performance of specified functions to persons possessing specified qualifications or experience.

7Regulating or prohibiting the employment in specified circumstances of all persons or any class of persons.

8(1)Requiring the making of arrangements for securing the health of persons at work or other persons, including arrangements for medical examinations and health surveys.

(2)Requiring the making of arrangements for monitoring the atmospheric or other conditions in which persons work.

9Imposing requirements with respect to any matter affecting the conditions in which persons work, including in particular such matters as the structural condition and stability of premises, the means of access to and egress from premises, cleanliness, temperature, fighting, ventilation, overcrowding, noise, vibrations, ionising and other radiations, dust and fumes.

10Securing the provision of specified welfare facilities for persons at work, including in particular such things as an adequate water supply, sanitary conveniences, washing and bathing facilities, ambulance and first-aid arrangements, cloakroom accommodation, sitting facilities and refreshment facilities.

11Imposing requirements with respect to the provision and use in specified circumstances of protective clothing or equipment, including clothing affording protection against the weather.

12Requiring in specified circumstances the taking of specified precautions in connection with the risk of fire.

13(1)Prohibiting or imposing requirements in connection with the emission into the atmosphere of any specified gas, smoke or dust or any other specified substance whatsoever.

(2)Prohibiting or imposing requirements in connection with the emission of noise, vibrations or any ionising or other radiations.

(3)Imposing requirements with respect to the monitoring of any such emission as is mentioned in the preceding sub-paragraphs.

14Imposing requirements with respect to the instruction, training and supervision of persons at work.

15(1)Requiring, in specified circumstances, specified matters to be notified in a specified manner to specified persons.

(2)Empowering inspectors in specified circumstances to require persons to submit written particulars of measures proposed to be taken to achieve compliance with any of the relevant statutory provisions.

16Imposing requirements with respect to the keeping and preservation of records and other documents, including plans and maps.

17Imposing requirements with respect to the management of animals.

18The following purposes as regards premises of any specified description where persons work, namely—

(a)requiring precautions to be taken against dangers to which the premises or persons therein are or may be exposed by reason of conditions (including natural conditions) existing in the vicinity;

(b)securing that persons in the premises leave them in specified circumstances.

19Conferring, in specified circumstances involving a risk of fire or explosion, power to search a person or any article which a person has with him for the purpose of ascertaining whether he has in his possession any article of a specified kind likely in those circumstances to cause a fire or explosion, and power to seize and dispose of any article of that kind found on such a search.

20Restricting, prohibiting or requiring the doing of any specified thing where any accident or other occurrence of a specified kind has occurred.

21As regards cases of any specified class, being a class such that the variety in .the circumstances of particular cases within it calls for the making of special provision for particular cases, any of the following purposes, namely—

(a)conferring on employers or other persons power to make rules or give directions with respect to matters affecting health or safety ;

(b)requiring employers or other persons to make rules with respect to any such matters ;

(c)empowering specified persons to require employers or other persons either to make rules with respect to any such matters or to modify any such rules previously made by virtue of this paragraph ; and

(d)making admissible in evidence without further proof, in such circumstances and subject to such conditions as may be specified, documents which purport to be copies of rules or rules of any specified class made under this paragraph.

22Conferring on any local or public authority power to make byelaws with respect to any specified matter, specifying the authority or person by whom any byelaws made in the exercise of that power need to be confirmed, and generally providing for the procedure to be followed in connection with the making of any such byelaws.

Interpretation

23(1)In this Schedule " specified " means specified in health and safety regulations.

(2)It is hereby declared that the mention in this Schedule of a purpose that falls within any more general purpose mentioned therein is without prejudice to the generality of the more general purpose.

Section 32.

SCHEDULE 4 MODIFICATIONS OF PART I IN CONNECTION WITH AGRICULTURE

Provisions applied	*Modifications*
1. Section 13(1) (various powers).	(a) Paragraph (b) shall be omitted;
	(b) references to the Commission or the Secretary of State shall be read as references to the appropriate Agriculture Minister, so however that references to the Commission's functions shall be read as references to the functions of that Minister under the relevant statutory provisions in relation to matters relating exclusively to the relevant agricultural purposes.
2. Section 14 (power to direct investigations and inquiries).	(a) References to the Commission shall be read as references to the appropriate Agriculture Minister;
	(b) in subsection (1), the reference to the general purposes of Part I shall be read as a reference to the relevant agricultural purposes;
	(c) in subsection (2), for the words from " direct " to " other " in paragraph (a) there shall be substituted the words " authorise any ", the words " with the consent of the Secretary of State " shall be omitted, and for the words from " only matters " to the end of the subsection there shall be substituted the words " matters relating exclusively to the relevant agricultural purposes ";

Provisions applied	*Modifications*
	(d) in subsection (6), references to the Secretary of State shall be read as references to the appropriate Agriculture Minister.
3. Section 16 (approval of codes of practice).	(a) In subsection (1), the reference to health and safety regulations shall be read as a reference to agricultural health and safety regulations and the words from " and except " to " agricultural operations " shall be omitted, but so that the section shall confer power to approve or issue codes of practice for any provision mentioned in section 16(1) only for the purposes of the application of that provision to matters relating exclusively to the relevant agricultural purposes;
	(b) a code of practice may either be approved for Great Britain and be so approved by the Minister of Agriculture, Fisheries and Food and the Secretary of State acting jointly, or be approved for England and Wales only and be so approved by that Minister or be approved for Scotland only and be so approved by the Secretary of State, and the references to the Commission shall accordingly be read as references to the Agriculture Ministers or the said Minister or the Secretary of State as the case may require;
	(c) for subsection (2) there shall be substituted—
	"(2)Before approving a code of practice under subsection (1) above the Minister or Ministers proposing to do so shall consult the Commission and any other body that appears to him or them to be appropriate.";
	(d)for subsection (5) there shall be substituted—

Provisions applied	Modifications
	"(5)The authority by whom a code of practice has been approved under this section may at any time withdraw approval from that code, but before doing so shall consult the same bodies as the authority would be required to consult under subsection (2) above if the authority were proposing to approve the code.".
4. Section 17(3) (use of approved codes in criminal proceedings).	The reference to the Commission shall be read as a reference to the Agriculture Ministers or either of them.
5. Section 27 (obtaining of information).	(a) References to the Commission or the Executive shall be read as references to the appropriate Agriculture Minister, so however that references to the Commission's functions shall be read as references to the functions of that Minister under the relevant statutory provisions in relation to matters relating exclusively to the relevant agricultural purposes; (b) references to an enforcing authority's functions shall be read as references to an enforcing authority's functions under the relevant statutory provisions in relation to matters relating exclusively to the relevant agricultural purposes; (c) in subsection (1), the words " with the consent of the Secretary of State " shall be omitted; (d) in subsection (2)(b), the reference to the Secretary of State shall be read as a reference to the appropriate Agriculture Minister, and the words " and the recipient of the information " shall be omitted.

SCHEDULE 5 SUBJECT-MATTER OF BUILDING REGULATIONS

1 Preparation of sites.

2 Suitability, durability and use of materials and components (including surface finishes).

3 Structural strength and stability, including—

(a) precautions against overloading, impact and explosion ;

(b) measures to safeguard adjacent buildings and services ;

(c) underpinning.

4 Fire precautions, including—

(a) structural measures to resist the outbreak and spread of fire and to mitigate its effects ;

(b) services, fittings and equipment designed to mitigate the effects of fire or to facilitate fire-fighting ;

(c) means of escape in case of fire and means for securing that such means of escape can be safely and effectively used at all material times.

5 Resistance to moisture and decay.

6 Measures affecting the transmission of heat

7 Measures affecting the transmission of sound.

8 Measures to prevent infestation.

9 Measures affecting the emission of smoke, gases, fumes, grit or dust or other noxious or offensive substances.

10 Drainage (including waste disposal units).

11 Cesspools and other means for the reception, treatment or disposal of foul matter.

12 Storage, treatment and removal of waste.

13 Installations utilising solid fuel, oil, gas, electricity or any other fuel or power (including appliances, storage tanks, heat exchangers, ducts, fans and other equipment).

14 Water services (including wells and bore-holes for the supply of water) and fittings and fixed equipment associated therewith.

15 Telecommunications services (including telephones and radio and television wiring installations).

16 Lifts, escalators, hoists, conveyors and moving footways.

17 Plant providing air under pressure.

18 Standards of heating, artificial lighting, mechanical ventilation and air-conditioning and provision of power outlets.

19 Open space about buildings and the natural lighting and ventilation of buildings.

20 Accommodation for specific purposes in or in connection with buildings, and the dimensions of rooms and other spaces within buildings.

21 Means of access to and egress from buildings and parts of buildings.

22 Prevention of danger and obstruction to persons in and about buildings (including passers-by).

23 Matters connected with or ancillary to any of the matters mentioned in the preceding provisions of this Schedule.

Section 61.

SCHEDULE 6 AMENDMENTS OF ENACTMENTS RELATING TO BUILDING REGULATIONS
PART I AMENDMENTS
Amendments of [1936 c. 49.] Public Health Act 1936

1 In section 64 of the 1936 Act (passing or rejection of plans)—

(a) for subsection (3) substitute—

"(3) Where plans of any proposed work deposited with a local authority are rejected in pursuance of the preceding provisions of this section, the person by whom or on whose behalf they were deposited may appeal against the rejection to the Secretary of State within the prescribed time and in the prescribed manner; and where the rejection results wholly or partly from the fact that a person or body whose approval or satisfaction in any respect is required by the regulations has withheld approval or not been satisfied, an appeal under this subsection may be brought on (or on grounds which include) the ground that the person or body in question ought in the circumstances to have approved or been satisfied in that respect."; and

(b) subsection (4) shall cease to have effect.

2 In section 65 of the 1936 Act (power to require removal or alteration of work not in conformity with building regulations etc.)—

(a) in subsection (1), after "therein" insert " and additions thereto and to execute such additional work in connection therewith ";

(b) after subsection (2) insert as subsection (2A)—

"(2A) Where a local authority have power to serve a notice under subsection (1) or (2) above on the owner of any work, they may in addition or instead serve such a notice on one or more of the following persons, namely the occupier and any builder or other person appearing to the authority to have control over the work.";

(c)in subsection (3), after " therein " insert " and additions thereto and execute such additional work in connection therewith " , and at the end add as a proviso—

"Provided that where a notice under subsection (1) or (2) above is given to two or more persons in pursuance of subsection (2A) above, then—

(a)if they are given the notices on different dates, the said period of twenty-eight days shall for each of them run from the later or latest of those dates; and

(b)if the notice is not complied with before the expiration of the said period or such longer period as a court of summary jurisdiction may on the application of any of them allow, any expenses recoverable as aforesaid may be recovered from any of them."; and

(d)in subsection (4), for " or subsection (2)" substitute " , (2) or (2A) " , and at the end add as a proviso—

"Provided that, in a case where plans were deposited nothing in this subsection shall be taken to prevent such a notice from being given (before the expiration of twelve months from the completion of the work in question) in respect of anything of which particulars were not required to be shown in the plans.".

3In section 90 of the 1936 Act (interpretation of Part II of that Act)—

(a)in subsection (2) (extended meaning, in that Part and building regulations, of references to the erection of a building), for the words from " and, so far " to " those regulations " substitute " except sections 61 to 71 and any other enactment to which section 74(1) of the Health and Safety at Work etc. Act 1974 applies "; and

(b)for subsection (3) (meaning of references to deposited plans) substitute—

"(3)In this Part of this Act, unless the context otherwise requires.—

(a)any reference to the deposit of plans in accordance with building regulations shall be construed as a reference to the deposit of plans in accordance with those regulations for the purposes of section 64 of this Act; and

(b)" plans" includes drawings of any other description and also specifications or other information in any form, and any reference to the deposit of plans shall be construed accordingly."

Amendments of [1961 c. 64.] Public Health Act 1961

4In section 4 of the 1961 Act (power to make building regulations)—

(a)in subsection (2) (power to make different provision for different areas) at the end add " and generally different provision for different circumstances or cases "; and

(b)in subsection (6) (penalties for contravening building regulations) after " building regulations" insert " other than a provision designated in the regulations as one to which this subsection does not apply, ", and for " one hundred pounds " and " ten pounds " substitute respectively " £400 " and "£50".

5In section 6 of the 1961 Act (power to dispense with or relax requirements of building regulations)—

(a)in subsection (1), add at the end the words " either unconditionally or subject to compliance with any conditions specified in the direction, being conditions with respect to matters directly connected with the dispensation or relaxation. ";

(b)in the proviso to subsection (2), for the words from " shall " onwards substitute " may except applications of any description ";

(c)for subsection (6) substitute—

"(6)An application by a local authority in connection with a building or proposed building in the area of that authority shall be made to the Secretary of State except where the power of giving the direction is exercisable by that authority.";

(d)after subsection (7), there shall be inserted as subsections (7A) and (7B)—

"(7A)If, on an application to the Secretary of State for a direction under this section, the Secretary of State considers that any requirement of building regulations to which the application relates is not applicable or is not or would not be contravened in the case of the work or proposed work to which the application relates, he may so determine and may give any directions that he considers necessary in the circumstances.

(7B)A person who contravenes any condition specified in a direction given under this section or permits any such condition to be contravened shall be liable to a fine not exceeding £400 and to a further fine not exceeding £50 for each day on which the offence continues after he is convicted. and";

(e)subsection (8) shall be omitted.

6In section 7 of the 1961 Act (appeal against local authority's refusal to dispense with or relax requirements of building regulations)—

(a)in subsection (1), after second " relax " insert " or grant such an application subject to conditions ", for " by notice in writing " substitute " in the prescribed manner ", for " one month" substitute " the prescribed period " and for " refusal" substitute " decision on the application ";

(b)in subsection (2), for the words from " a period " to " and the local authority " substitute " the prescribed period ";

(c)subsections (3) to (6) shall be omitted ; and

(d)at the end there shall be added the following subsection:—

"(7)Section 6(7A) of this Act shall apply in relation to an appeal to the Secretary of State under this section as it applies in relation to an application to him for a direction under section 6.".

7For section 8 of the 1961 Act (advertisement of proposal to relax building regulations) substitute—

"8Opportunity to make representations about proposal to relax building regulations.

(1)Before the Secretary of State or a local authority give a direction under section 6 of this Act the prescribed steps shall be taken for affording to persons likely to be affected by the direction an opportunity to make representations about it; and before giving the direction the Secretary of State or, as the case may be, the local authority shall consider any representations duly made in accordance with the regulations.

(2)Building regulations—

(a)may make provision as to the time to be allowed for making representations under the preceding subsection ;

(b)may require an applicant for such a direction, as a condition that his application shall be entertained, to pay or undertake to pay the cost of publishing any notice which is required by the regulations to be published in connection with the application; and

(c)may exclude the requirements of the preceding subsection in prescribed cases.".

8In section 9(3) of the 1961 Act (consultation with Building Regulations Advisory Committee and other bodies before making building regulations), at the end add " (including in particular, as regards regulations relevant to any of their functions, the National Water Council). ".

PART II[1936 C. 49.] PUBLIC HEALTH ACT 1936 SECTION 65 AND [1961 C. 64.] PUBLIC HEALTH ACT 1961 SECTIONS 4, 6 AND 7 AS AMENDED

The Public Health Act 1936

65(1)If any work to which building regulations are applicable contravenes any of those regulations, the authority, without prejudice to their right to take proceedings for a fine in respect of the contravention, may by notice require the owner either to pull down or remove the work or, if he so elects, to effect such alterations therein and additions thereto and to execute such additional work in connection therewith as may be necessary to make it comply with the regulations.

(2)If, in a case where the local authority are by any section of this Act other than the last preceding section expressly required or authorised to reject plans, any work to which building regulations are applicable is executed either without plans having been deposited, or notwithstanding the rejection of the plans, or otherwise than in accordance with any requirements subject to which the authority passed the plans, the authority may by notice to the owner either require him to pull down or remove the work, or require him either to pull down or remove the work or, if he so elects, to comply with any other requirements specified in the notice, being requirements which they might have made under the section in question as a condition of passing plans.

(2A)Where a local authority have power to serve a notice under subsection (1) or (2) above on the owner of any work, they may in addition or instead serve such a notice on one or more of the following persons, namely the occupier and any builder or other person appearing to the authority to have control over the work.

(3)If a person to whom a notice has been given under the foregoing provisions of this section fails to comply with the notice before the expiration of twenty-eight days, or such longer period as a court of summary jurisdiction may on his application allow, the local authority may pull down or remove the work in question, or effect such alterations therein and additions thereto and execute such additional work in connection therewith as they deem necessary, and may recover from him the expenses reasonably incurred by them in so doing:

Provided that where a notice under subsection (1) or (2) above is given to two or more persons in pursuance of subsection (2A) above, then—

(a)if they are given the notices on different dates, the said period of twenty-eight days shall for each of them run from the later or latest of those dates ; and

(b)if the notice is not complied with before the expiration of the said period or such longer period as a court of summary jurisdiction may on the application of any of them allow, any expenses recoverable as aforesaid may be recovered from any of them.

(4)No such notice as is mentioned in subsection (1), (2) or (2A) of this section shall be given after the expiration of twelve months from the date of the completion of the work in question, and, in any case where plans were deposited, it shall not be open to the authority to give such a notice on the ground that the work contravenes any building regulation or, as the case may be, does not comply with their requirements under any such section of this Act as aforesaid, if either the plans were passed by the authority, or notice of their rejection was not given within the prescribed period from the deposit thereof, and if the work has been executed in accordance with the plans and of any requirement made by the local authority as a condition of passing the plans:

Provided that, in a case where plans were deposited, nothing in this subsection shall be taken to prevent such a notice from being given (before the expiration of twelve months from the completion of the work in question) in respect of anything of which particulars were not required to be shown in the plans.

(5)Nothing in this section shall affect the right of a local authority, or of the Attorney-General, or any other person, to apply for an injunction for the removal or alteration of any work on the ground that it contravenes any regulation or any enactment in this Act, but if the work is one in respect of which plans were deposited and the plans were passed by the local authority, or notice of their rejection was not given within the prescribed period after the deposit thereof, and if the work has been executed in accordance with the plans, the court on granting an injunction shall have power to order the local authority to pay to the owner of the work such compensation as the court thinks just, but before making any such order the court shall in accordance with rules of court cause the local authority, if not a party to the proceedings, to be joined as a party thereto.

The [1961 c. 64.] Public Health Act 1961

4(1). . . . .

(2)Any provision contained in building regulations may be made so as to apply generally, or in an area specified in the regulations, and the regulations may make different provision for different areas and generally different provision for different circumstances or cases.

(3)It shall be the function of every local authority to enforce building regulations in their district.

(4)Local authorities shall, in relation to building regulations, have all such functions under sections 64 and 65 of the [1936 c. 49.] Public Health Act 1936 (which confer power to pass plans, and to enforce building byelaws) as they have in relation to building byelaws.

(5)Building regulations may include such supplemental and incidental provisions as appear to the Secretary of State to be expedient.

(6)If a person contravenes or fails to comply with any provision contained in building regulations, other than a provision designated in the regulations as one to which this subsection does not apply, he shall be liable to a fine not exceeding £400 and to a further fine not exceeding £50 for each day on which the default continues after he is convicted.

(7)The power of making building regulations shall be exercisable by statutory instrument which shall be subject to annulment in pursuance of a resolution of either House of Parliament.

6(1)Subject to the provisions of this section, if the Secretary of State, on an application made in accordance with the provisions of this Act, considers that the operation of any requirement in building regulations would be unreasonable in relation to the particular case to which the application relates, he may after consultation with the local authority, give a direction dispensing with or relaxing that requirement either unconditionally or subject to compliance with any conditions specified in the direction, being conditions with respect to matters directly connected with the dispensation or relaxation.

(2)If building regulations so provide as regards any requirement contained in the regulations, the power to dispense with or relax that requirement under subsection (1) of this section shall be exercisable by the local authority (instead of by the Secretary of State after consultation with the local authority):

Provided that any building regulations made by virtue of this subsection may except applications of any description.

(3)Building regulations may provide as regards any requirement contained in the regulations that the foregoing subsections of this section shall not apply.

(4)An application under this section shall be in such form ....and shall contain such particulars as may be................................ prescribed.

(5)The application shall be made to the local authority and, except where the power of giving the direction is exercisable by the local authority, the local authority shall at once transmit the application to the Secretary of State and give notice to the applicant that it has been so transmitted.

(6)An application by a local authority in connection with a building or proposed building in the area of that authority shall be made to the Secretary of State except where the power of giving the direction is exercisable by that authority.

(7)The provisions of Part I of the First Schedule to this Act shall have effect as regards any application made under this section for a direction which will affect the application of building regulations to work which has been carried out before the making of the application.

(7A)If, on an application to the Secretary of State for a direction under this section, the Secretary of State considers that any requirement of building regulations to which the application relates is not applicable or is not or would not be contravened in the case of the work or proposed work to which the application relates he may so determine and may give any directions that he considers necessary in the circumstances.

(7B)A person who contravenes any condition specified in a direction given under this section or permits any such condition to be contravened shall be liable to a fine not exceeding £400 and to a further fine not exceeding £50 for each day on which the offence continues after he is convicted.

7(1)If a local authority refuse an application to dispense with or relax any requirement in building regulations which they have power to dispense with or relax, or grant such an applicatiion subject to conditions, the applicant may in the prescribed manner appeal to the Secretary of State within the prescribed period from the date on which the local authority notify the applicant of their decision on the application.

(2)If within the prescribed period the local authority do not notify the applicant of their decision on the application, subsection (1) of this section shall appply in relation to the application as if the local authority had refused the application and notified the applicant of their decision at the end of the said period.

. . . .

(7)Section 6(7A) of this Act shall apply in relation to an appeal to the Secretary of State under this section as it applies in relation to an application to him for a direction under section 6.

Section 75.

SCHEDULE 7 AMENDMENTS OF [1959 c. 24.] BUILDING (SCOTLAND) ACT 1959

1 In section 3 (building standards regulations)—

(a)in subsection (2), after the words "health, safety" there shall be inserted the word " welfare ", and at the end there shall be added the words " and for furthering the conservation of fuel and power ";

(b)in subsection (3), there shall be added the words—

"(d)be framed to any extent by reference to a document published by or on behalf of the Secretary of State or any other person.";

(c)at the end of the section there shall be added the following subsection—

"(7)The Secretary of State may by order made by statutory instrument repeal or modify any enactment to which this subsection applies if it appears to him that the enactment is inconsistent with, or is unnecessary or requires alteration in consequence of, any provision contained in the building standards regulations.

This subsection applies to any enactment contained in any Act passed before or in the same Session as the Health and Safety at Work etc. Act 1974 other than an enactment contained in the Building (Scotland) Act 1959."

2 In section 4 (relaxation of building standards regulations)—

(a)for subsection (5) there shall be substituted the following subsections—

"(5)A direction under subsection (1)(b) above—

(a)shall, if it so provides, cease to have effect at the end of such period as may be specified in the direction ;

276

(b)may be varied or revoked by a subsequent direction of the Secretary of State.

(5A)If at any time a direction under subsection (1)(b) above ceases to have effect by virtue of subsection (5)(a) above or is varied or revoked under subsection (5)(b) above, that fact shall not affect the continued operation of the direction (with any conditions specified therein) in any case in which before that time an application for a warrant in connection with the construction or change of use of a building, part or all of which is of the class to which the direction relates, was, in accordance with regulations made under section 2 of this Act, lodged with a buildings authority.";

(b)in subsections (6) and (7), after the words " subsection (1)(b)" there shall be inserted the words " or (5)(&) ";

(c)after subsection (7) there shall be inserted the following subsection :—

"(7A)A person making an application under subsection (1)(b) above shall pay to the Secretary of State such fee as may be prescribed ; and regulations made by virtue of this subsection may prescribe different fees for different cases:

Provided that the Secretary of State may in any particular case remit the whole or part of any fee payable by virtue of this subsection.".

3After section 4A, there shall be inserted the following section—

"4BPower of Secretary of State to approve types of building, etc.

(1)The following provisions of this section shall have effect with a view to enabling the Secretary of State, either on an application made to him in that behalf or of his own accord, to approve any particular type of building as conforming, either generally or in any class of case, to particular provisions of the building standards regulations.

(2)An application for the approval under this section of a type of building shall be made in the prescribed manner.

(3)Where under subsection (1) above the Secretary of State approves a type of building as conforming to particular provisions of the building standards regulations either generally or in any class of case, he may issue a certificate to that effect specifying—

(a)the type of building to which the certificate relates;

(b)the provisions of the building standards regulations to which the certificate relates ; and

(c)where applicable, the class or classes of case to which the certificate applies.

(4)A certificate under this section shall, if it so provides, cease to have effect at the end of such period as may be specified in the certificate.

(5)If, while a certificate under this section is in force, it is found, in any particular case involving a building of the type to which the certificate relates, that the building in question is of that type and the case is one to which the certificate applies, that building shall in that particular case be deemed to conform to the provisions of the building standards regulations to which the certificate relates.

(6)The Secretary of State may from time to time vary a certificate under this section either on an application made to him in that behalf or of his own accord ; but in the case of a certificate issued on an application made by a person under subsection (1) above, the Secretary of State, except where he varies it on the application of that person, shall before varying it give that person reasonable notice that he proposes to do so.

(7)A person making an application under subsection (1) or (6) above shall pay to the Secretary of State such fee as may be prescribed ; and regulations made by virtue of this subsection may prescribe different fees for different cases:

Provided that the Secretary of State may in any particular case remit the whole or part of any fee payable by virtue of this subsection.

(8)The Secretary of State may at any time revoke a certificate issued under this section, but before doing so shall give the person, if any, on whose application the certificate was issued reasonable notice that he proposes to do so.

(9)Where the Secretary of State issues a certificate under this section or varies or revokes a certificate so issued, he shall publish notice of that fact in such manner as he thinks fit.

(10)If at any time a certificate under this section ceases to have effect by virtue of subsection (4) above or is varied or revoked under the preceding provisions of this section, that fact shall not affect the continued operation of subsection (5) above by virtue of that certificate in any case in which before that time an application for a warrant in connection with the construction of a type of building to which the certificate relates was, in accordance with regulations made under section 2 of this Act, lodged with a buildings authority.

(11)For the purposes of subsection (3) above or any variation of a certificate under subsection (6) above, a class of case may be framed in any way that the Secretary of State thinks fit."

4In section 6 (application of building standards regulations and building operations regulations to construction or demolition, and to change of use, of buildings)—

(a)after subsection (3) there shall be inserted the following subsection—

"(3A)Notwithstanding that a buildings authority are not satisfied that the information submitted to them with an application for a warrant for the construction of a building is sufficient in respect of such stage in the construction as may be prescribed to show that the building when constructed will not fail to conform to the building standards regulations, they may grant a warrant for the construction of the building but subject to the condition that work on such prescribed stage shall not be proceeded with until such further information relating to that stage as they may require is submitted to them and until they have made an amendment to the terms of the warrant authorising such work to proceed:

Provided that they shall, subject to subsection (8) of this section, make such an amendment on application being made therefor in the prescribed manner only if they are satisfied that nothing in the information submitted to them in respect of the prescribed stage shows that that stage when constructed will fail to conform to the building standards regulations.";

(b)in subsection (10), after the words " any such " there shall be inserted the words " prescribed stage as is mentioned in subsection (3A) of this section and any such ".

5In section 9 (certificates of completion)—

(a)in subsection (2), for the words " but only if, they are satisfied that" there shall be substituted the words " , so far as they are able to ascertain after taking all reasonable steps in that behalf, ";

(b)in subsection (3), for the words, " be satisfied as mentioned in the last foregoing subsection " there shall be substituted the words " grant a certificate of completion ";

(c)after subsection (3) there shall be inserted the following subsection—

"(3A)In respect of so much of a building as consists of such an installation as may be prescribed, not being an electrical installation, a buildings authority shall not grant a certificate of completion unless there is produced to them a certificate granted by a person of such class as may be prescribed certifying that the installation complies with such of the said conditions as relate to it:

Provided that this subsection shall not apply in a case where it is shown to the satisfaction of the buildings authority that for some reasonable cause such a certificate cannot be produced.";

(d)in subsection (4) for the words " the last foregoing subsection " there shall be substituted the words " subsection (3) or (3A) above ".

6In section 11(1)(b) (power of local authorities to require buildings to conform to building standards regulations), after the words " health, safety " there shall be inserted the word " welfare ", and after the word " generally " there shall be inserted the words " and for furthering the conservation of fuel and power ".

7In section 19 (penalties), for the words " ten pounds " and " one hundred pounds ", wherever they occur, there shall be substituted respectively the words " £50 " and " £400 ".

8After section 19 there shall be inserted the following section—

"19ACivil liability

(1)Subject to the provisions of this section, a breach to which this section applies shall, so far as it causes damage, be actionable except in so far as may be otherwise prescribed ; and in any action brought by virtue of this subsection such defence as may be prescribed shall be available.

(2)This section applies to the following breaches—

(a)failure to comply with the terms or conditions of a warrant for the construction, demolition or change of use of a building or with any order under this Act relating to the construction of a building;

(b)contravention of any provision of the building operations regulations ;

(c)constructing a building without a warrant otherwise than in accordance with the building standards regulations ;

(d)changing the use of a building without a warrant where after the change of use the building does not conform to so much of the building standards regulations as become applicable, or apply more onerously, to the building by reason of the change of use.

(3)Subsection (1) above and any defence provided for in regulations made by virtue thereof shall not apply in the case of a breach to which this section applies in connection with a building erected before the date on which that subsection comes into force unless the breach arises in relation to the change of use, extension, alteration, demolition, repair, maintenance or fitting of such a building.

(4)Nothing in this section shall be construed as affecting the extent (if any) to which a breach to which this section applies is actionable in a case to which subsection (1) above does not apply, or as prejudicing any right of action which exists apart from the provisions of this section.

(5)In this section " damage" includes the death of, or injury to, any person (including any disease and any impairment of a person's physical or mental condition)."

9In section 26 (Crown rights)—

(a)in subsection (1) after the words " Crown and " there shall be inserted the words " subject to the provisions of this section ";

(b)after subsection (2) there shall be inserted the following subsections—

"(2A)The building standards regulations shall, except in so far as they otherwise prescribe, apply to a Crown building as they would apply if the building were not a Crown building.

(2B)A Crown building to which the building standards regulations apply shall be constructed in accordance with those regulations.

(2C)Any extension to or alteration of a Crown building to which the building standards regulations apply or would apply on the extension or alteration of the building shall not cause the building as extended or altered, as a direct result of the extension or, as the case may be, the alteration—

(a)if it conformed to the building standards regulations immediately before the date of commencement of the operations, to fail to conform to them ; or

(b)if it failed to conform to the building standards regulations immediately before that date, to fail to conform to them to a greater degree than that to which it failed to conform immediately before that date ;

and any change of use of a Crown building shall not cause the building after the change of use to fail to conform to so much of the building standards regulations as will become applicable, or will apply more onerously, to the building by reason of the change of use.

(2D)Section 19A of this Act shall apply to a Crown building as it applies to a building other than a Crown building, but as if for subsection (2) there were substituted the following subsection:—

"(2)A breach to which this section applies is a failure to comply with subsection (2B) or (2C) of section 26 of this Act or a contravention of any provision of the building operations regulations".

(2E)Without prejudice to any case to which proviso (a) to subsection (1) above is applicable, the Secretary of State shall have the like powers of dispensing with or relaxing the provisions of the building standards regulations in relation to a Crown building as he has under section 4(1) of this Act in relation to a building other than a Crown building ; and subsections (3), (4), (5), (5A) and (9) of the said section 4 shall apply for the purposes of this section as if—

(a)in subsection (4), the words " or, as the case maybe, the buildings authority " were omitted ;

(b)in subsection (5A), for the words from " an application " to the end there were substituted the words " the construction or change of use of a building, part or all of which is of the class to which the direction relates, was begun ";

(c)in subsection (9), the words "or section 4A(3) of this Act" were omitted.

(2F)Without prejudice to any case to which the said proviso is applicable, in the application of section 4B of this Act to a Crown building, subsection (10) shall have effect as if for the words from " an application " to the end there were substituted the words " the construction of a building, part or all of which is of the type to which the certificate relates, was begun.".

Section 78.

SCHEDULE 8TRANSITIONAL PROVISIONS WITH RESPECT TO [1961 C. 34.] FIRE CERTIFICATES UNDER FACTORIES ACT 1961 OR [1963 C. 41.] OFFICES, SHOPS AND RAILWAY PREMISES ACT 1963

1In this Schedule—

- " the 1971 Act " means the [1971 c. 40.] Fire Precautions Act 1971 ;

- " 1971 Act certificate" means a fire certificate within the meaning of the 1971 Act;

- " Factories Act certificate " means a certificate under section 40 of the [1961 c. 34.] Factories Act 1961 (means of escape in case of fire-certification by fire authority);

- " Offices Act certificate" means a fire certificate under section 29 of the [1963 c. 41.] Offices, Shops and Railway Premises Act 1963.

2(1)Where by virtue of an order under section 1 of the 1971 Act a 1971 Act certificate becomes required in respect of any premises at a time when there is in force in respect of those premises a Factories Act certificate or an Offices Act certificate (" the existing certificate"), the following provisions of this paragraph shall apply.

(2)The existing certificate shall continue in force (irrespective of whether the section under which it was issued remains in force) and—

(a)shall as from the said time be deemed to be a 1971 Act certificate validly issued with respect to the premises with respect to which it was issued and to cover the use or uses to which those premises were being put at that time; and

(b)may (in particular) be amended, replaced or revoked in accordance with the 1971 Act accordingly.

(3)Without prejudice to sub-paragraph (2)(b) above, the existing certificate, as it has effect by virtue of sub-paragraph (2) above, shall as from the said time be treated as imposing in relation to the premises the like requirements as were previously imposed in relation thereto by the following provisions, that is to say—

(a)if the existing certificate is a Factories Act certificate, the following provisions of the Factories Act 1961, namely sections 41(1), 48 (except subsections (5), (8) and (9)), 49(1), 51(1) and 52(1) and (4) and, so far as it relates to a proposed increase in the number of persons employed in any premises, section 41(3);

(b)if the existing certificate is an Offices Act certificate the following provisions of the Offices, Shops and Railway Premises Act 1963, namely sections 30(1), 33, 34(1) and (2), 36(1) and 38(1) and, so far as it relates to a proposed increase in the number of persons employed to work in any premises at any one time, section 30(3).

3Any application for a Factories Act certificate or an Offices Act certificate with respect to any premises which is pending at the time when by virtue of an order under section 1 of the 1971 Act a 1971 Act certificate becomes required in respect of those premises shall be deemed to be an application for a 1971 Act certificate in respect of them duly made in accordance with the 1971 Act and may be proceeded with accordingly; but (without prejudice to section 5(2) of the 1971 Act) the fire authority may, as a condition of proceeding with such an application, require the applicant to specify any matter or give them any information which would ordinarily have been required by section 5(1) of that Act.

Section 83.

SCHEDULE 9 MINOR AND CONSEQUENTIAL AMENDMENTS

[1926 c. 59.] The Coroners (Amendment) Act 1926

1 In section 13(2)(c) of the Coroners (Amendment) Act 1926 (by virtue of which an inquest must be held with a jury in cases of death from certain causes of which notice is required to be given to any inspector or other officer of a government department), after the words "of a government department" there shall be inserted the words " or to an inspector appointed under section 19 of the Health and Safety at Work etc. Act 1974 ".

[1957 c. 20.] The House of Commons Disqualification Act 1957

2 In Part II of Schedule 1 to the House of Commons Disqualification Act 1957 (which specifies bodies of which all members are disqualified under that Act), as it applies to the House of Commons of the Parliament of the United Kingdom, there shall be inserted at the appropriate place in alphabetical order the words " The Health and Safety Commission ".

[1967 c. 13.] The Parliamentary Commissioner Act 1967

3 In Schedule 2 to the Parliamentary Commissioner Act 1967 (which lists the authorities subject to investigation under that Act) there shall be inserted in the appropriate places in alphabetical order the words " Health and Safety Commission " and " Health and Safety Executive ".

Section 83.

SCHEDULE 10REPEALS

Chapter	Short Title	Extent of Repeal
26 Geo. 5 & 1 Edw. 8. c. 49.	The Public Health Act 1936.	Section 53. Section 64(4) and (5). In section 67, the words from " and the Secretary of State's decision " to the end of the section. Section 71. In section 343(1), the definition of " building regulations ".
7 & 8 Geo. 6. c. 31.	The Education Act 1944.	Section 63(1).
10 & 11 Geo. 6. c. 51.	The Town and Country Planning Act 1947.	In Schedule 8, the amendment of section 53 of the Public Health Act 1936.
2 & 3 Eliz. 2. c. 32.	The Atomic Energy Authority Act 1954.	Section 5(5).
4 & 5 Eliz. 2. c. 52.	The Clean Air Act 1956.	Section 24.
9 & 10 Eliz. 2. c. 64.	The Public Health Act 1961.	In section 4, subsection (1) and, in subsection (4), the words from " and building " to the end of the subsection. In section 6, in subection (4), the words " as may be prescribed by building

Chapter	Short Title	Extent of Repeal
		regulations " and the word " so ", and subsection (8).
		Section 7(3) to (6).
		Section 10(1) and (2).
		In Schedule 1, in Part III, the amendments of sections 53,61, 62 and 71 of the Public Health Act 1936 and, in the amendments of the Clean Air Act 1956, the amendment of section 24 and the word " twenty-four" in the last paragraph.
1965 c. 16.	The Airports Authority Act 1965.	In section 19(3), the words from " and section 71 " to " regulations) " and the words " and the proviso to the said section 71 ".
1971 c. 40.	The Fire Precautions Act 1971.	In section 2, paragraphs (a) to (c). Section 11. In section 17(1)(i), the word " and " where last occurring. In section 43(1), the definition of " building regulations ".
1971 c. 75.	The Civil Aviation Act 1971.	In Schedule 5, in paragraph 2(1), the words from " and section 71 " to " regulations)" and the words " and the proviso to the said section 71 ".

Chapter	Short Title	Extent of Repeal
1972 c. 28.	The Employment Medical Advisory Service Act 1972.	Sections 1 and 6. Schedule 1.
1972 c. 58.	The National Health Service (Scotland) Act 1972.	In Schedule 6, paragraph 157.
1972 c. 70.	The Local Government Act 1972.	In Schedule 14, paragraph 43.
1973 c. 32.	The National Health Service Reorganisation Act 1973.	In Schedule 4, paragraph 137.
1973 c. 50.	The Employment and Training Act 1973.	In Schedule 3, paragraph 14.
1973 c. 64.	The Maplin Development Act 1973.	In Schedule 2, in paragraph 2(1), the words from " and section 71" to " regulations) ".

About the Author

An established health and safety practitioner, I started my career in the manufacturing industry as a machine operator, back in a time which too many of us remember where health and safety was seen as simply being told to "Watch yourself!"

Taking the NEBOSH route to competency, I first became a safety officer, before progressing to safety manager, dealing with the accidents and incidents that were all too inherent of the time.

An opportunity arose to change industries into vocational health and safety training for the emergency services, a position that very quickly provided vast exposure to multiple disciplines and risk management, which would have never been experienced in manufacturing.

I have had the pleasure of working with the Fire Rescue Service and NHS Hazardous Area Response Teams (HART) and spent two years as a visiting lecturer at Morton Fire College, and can say, hand on heart, I learned more from them than they ever did from me.

I have spent over 15 years with the Mines Rescue Service, training well in excess of 1000 individuals in confined spaces, first aid, working at height, rescue and recovery, and my personal favourite, safety management.

I have worked on large scale projects in most industries such as power, utilities, oil and gas including off-shore and internationally. Often acting as a consultant, I have dealt with many client management issues including improvement notices, and throughout, I have tried my best to make safety management accessible, understandable, and as "Common Sense" as possible. This is the ethos of my books, to provide clear understanding of the requirements of legislation to allow others to ensure their workplaces are safe and without risk to their employees.